"This book is raw and personal as [...] pursuit of the truth that heals. Get [...] of hope through her grace-infused insights."

Craig Groeschel, pastor of Life.Church
and *New York Times* bestselling author

Amy Groeschel, cofounder of Life.Church
and founder of Branch15

"This book isn't written with theories, nice sentiments, or cute ideas. Landra wrote this book from a tear-soaked place of pain and loss and heartache—the same place you might be in right now. In *Where Is God in This?* you will not only find her hard-earned insight, biblical wisdom, and encouragement but also a friend who will sit with you in the pain, ask the hard questions, and hold your hand on the journey. If you're ready to grow your roots down deep and open your heart for God to bring purpose out of your pain, this book is for you!"

Jennie Lusko, cofounder of Fresh Life Church
and bestselling author

"If you've ever wondered where God is during the dark moments of life, this book is for you. Landra begins her story with the devastating loss of her sister LeeBeth. We have had the honor of knowing both Landra and LeeBeth personally, so watching their family process LeeBeth's death was heartbreakingly beautiful. It was a true testament to their faith and inspired our own faith in such a profound way. Landra invites you on that journey—one that is still in progress—and she offers hope in knowing that God leverages our pain for good, if we allow him to. *Where Is God in This?* is a timely reminder that no matter our circumstances, no matter what's going on in the world around us, we are still held by the Creator of the universe. And he will never leave us or forsake us. Walking side by side both gratitude and grief is something God has modeled for us and something Landra and her family continue to model through this journey of faith."

Sean and Catherine Lowe, television personalities

"People like stories with happy endings. We want to hear about how good life is after the battle, but that's not what Landra Young Hughes does in *Where Is God in This?* She is right in the middle of one of the most painful experiences of her life—grieving the death of her sister. She writes with the authority of someone standing in the center of the firefight. The pain is fresh, but so is the faith."

Jimmy Evans, founder and president of XO Marriage

WHERE
IS
GOD
IN
THIS?

WHERE
IS
GOD
IN
THIS?

LOOKING FOR GOD'S GOODNESS
IN OUR STRUGGLES

LANDRA YOUNG HUGHES
WITH HOLLY CRAWSHAW

BakerBooks

a division of Baker Publishing Group
Grand Rapids, Michigan

Published by Baker Books
a division of Baker Publishing Group
PO Box 6287, Grand Rapids, MI 49516-6287
www.bakerbooks.com

Printed in the United States of America

Library of Congress Cataloging-in-Publication Data
Names: Hughes, Landra Young, 1994– author. | Crawshaw, Holly, other.
Title: Where is God in this? : looking for God's goodness in our struggles / Landra Young Hughes ; with Holly Crawshaw.
Description: Grand Rapids, MI : Baker Books, a division of Baker Publishing Group, [2022] | Includes bibliographical references.
Identifiers: LCCN 2022004272 | ISBN 9780801094842 (paperback) | ISBN 9781540902580 (casebound) | ISBN 9781493432912 (ebook)
Subjects: LCSH: Peace of mind—Religious aspects—Christianity. | God (Christianity)—Goodness.
Classification: LCC BV4908.5 .H83 2022 | DDC 248.4—dc23/eng/20220303
LC record available at https://lccn.loc.gov/2022004272

The author is represented by The FEDD Agency, Inc.

Baker Publishing Group publications use paper produced from sustainable forestry practices and post-consumer waste whenever possible.

22 23 24 25 26 27 28   7 6 5 4 3 2 1

In memory of my sister LeeBeth Young,
whose beautiful life continues to teach us
all about God's good purpose.

CONTENTS

1

God? I'd Like to Speak to the Manager

I have told you these things, so that in me you may have peace. In this world you will have trouble. But take heart! I have overcome the world.

John 16:33 NIV

I'm not really OK.

That's probably *not* how you should start a book that's supposed to help people, right? Especially a book about finding value in the struggles and suffering we experience in life. I should probably open with a lighthearted story you can connect with. Something that would engage you, maybe make you smile—something endearing, almost kitschy. The decline of the *Bachelor* franchise would be an obvious choice.

But that's not what we're doing in this book.

See, I'm in the middle of what has to be the most soul-draining season of my life. And right now, it feels dark. It feels heavy. And it feels hopeless.

Notice, I said it *feels*. Because you know the thing about feelings? They're not always a representation of what's *true*. And this knowledge *does* assuage the ache slightly, but for the most part, I vacillate between crushing waves of despair and blurry interludes of business as usual.

On January 18, 2021, my precious sister LeeBeth Young died.

LeeBeth was sick. She had been sick for a long time but not the kind of sick that means Get Well Soon balloons and all-you-can-eat ice cream. LeeBeth was an alcoholic—a binge drinker. Now, if you're not familiar with the disease of addiction, I'm sure it's impossible to wrap your head around the idea that someone can't stop doing the thing that makes them sicker. But that's the nature of the mental insanity that seizes those of us with this particular thorn.

I say "us," because as an anorexic/bulimic in recovery, I have a level of empathy for LeeBeth. By God's miraculous grace, I walk in healing from my addiction. And by the same miraculous grace, LeeBeth is in heaven with our Father, walking out her healing with a restored mind and body.

Yes, there's the glorious and life-giving hope of heaven. But here on earth, it still hurts.

It had only been a few short years since we realized Lee-Beth was a full-blown alcoholic. She never partied growing up. She never drank. She didn't sleep around. In fact, she was pretty perfect by surface standards. But later in life, LeeBeth suffered from loneliness and depression, which transformed her into someone completely different (more on this later).

When LeeBeth was sick, it was like she had undergone a total personality transplant. I didn't even know my sister the last few months leading up to her death.

I'd like to paint some pretty picture for you here and say we had a meaningful moment in her final days that I look back on now as some mysterious treasure, but that's not the case. Death rarely gives you that perfect Pixar ending.

I did have a chance to talk to LeeBeth shortly before she died. And I guess if I were going to look back and say there was one last time we connected meaningfully, that would be it. She called me from my dad's phone and just kept repeating over and over how sorry she was for being sick again.

"I just want you better," I told her. "I love you. My kids love you. We all love you. We just want LeeBeth back."

I was so angry that night. I asked my husband, Brad, "When is she going to hit rock bottom? When will she lose more than she's willing to lose and make some sort of change? Why does she keep doing this to us? To herself? What is it going to take for her to get well?"

Kind and brilliant Brad said, "Landra, I think what she really needs from us is just acceptance. No more advice, no more telling her what to do. She just really needs to know that we're beside her on this journey. That we love her no matter what."

If you have a significant other, is there anything more annoying than when they're calm, rational, *and* right when you just want to be mad?

But he was. He was right. LeeBeth just needed our love.

I'd like to think the last memory LeeBeth has of this earth is of her father, holding her, caring for her, telling her how much he loved her. Dad was in his office working on a sermon—a message about God asking Abraham to sacrifice his son Isaac—when he heard a noise down the hallway.

LeeBeth was having a seizure. My brother and sister-in-law were staying there for the night, and Dad screamed for them to start CPR while he called 911. The paramedics who arrived were able to find a faint heartbeat, but no pulse. What happened next is a hazy, bitter blur.

Intubation.

Doctors.

My dad trying to fly my mom back home.

Calls.

Texts.

Prayers.

Tears.

Hearts shattering.

"I'm sorry," the doctor finally said. "There's nothing else left for us to do. LeeBeth is gone."

Some of us in the room and some of us on FaceTime watched in utter disbelief as they disconnected my beautiful, so-much-life-to-live, thirty-four-year-old sister from the machines keeping her body alive.

My mom, watching from a cold chair in an airport sitting area, sobbed. Her anguish, her desperation, the cries of a mother torn apart—I'll never forget it. It was the darkest moment of my life.

There are people in this world who abuse their bodies to no end. I know, because there was a time I abused my own by starving it. There are people who use lethal amounts of drugs, who drink, who inject or snort or take anything put in their hands. They get to live, but LeeBeth does not. This is a truth. This is a fact. But how I choose to process this data is up to me. Some days, I do well with it. Others . . . I don't.

I have a daughter of my own—Sterling. She's perfect. And I love her so much it is literally painful.

Have you ever asked your kid, "What's something Mommy [or Daddy] says all the time?" Be careful if you do because kids don't lie about stuff like this. When we posed this question to Sterling, without hesitation her response was, "Mommy says, no, no, no, no!" (complete with a full-on finger wag). In fact, I'm pretty sure that *no* was Sterling's first word. It's cute when a toddler says it. But when God says it?

It doesn't feel cute.

If you've been told no by God before, you can relate (pretty sure that's all of us). When God doesn't answer our prayers the way we want, when something feels unfair or unjust, when bad things happen, when we're disappointed, stuck, hurt, or angry, it can feel an awful lot like God has stopped caring about us. In fact, it can sometimes feel like God is on the opposite team or like we're being punished. And we start thinking and searching and rehashing our actions, wondering which of our many sins is the reason we are suffering.

The problem with that way of thinking is just that—it's *our* way of thinking. It's our human logic trying to reason out how an omniscient, all-powerful God operates, and that is like explaining physics to a newborn. We cannot wrap our minds around the infinite power of the almighty Creator. But we like to try. And we also like to give him feedback when things don't go the way we think they should.

If you break it down, if you bring our experiences of adversity and struggle into the light of God's Word, it would be more surprising if we *didn't* face difficulty. I mean, aren't we promised as much? John 16:33 says, "I have told you these things, so that in me you may have peace. In this world you will have trouble. But take heart! I have overcome the world" (NIV).

"In this world *you will have trouble.*" This is 100 percent the truth.

"But take heart! *I have overcome the world.*" This is also 100 percent the truth.

I think one of the greatest tensions of the Christian walk is reconciling our fallen world with a loving Father. But we quickly forget that this world is not the world God created. Genesis 1:31 tells us, "God saw everything he had made. And it was very good."

The earth God made was not just good—it was *very* good. God walked side by side with humankind. Nothing separated him from us and us from him. There were no strokes, no heart attacks, no cancer, and no alcoholism in the world God created. But you've heard what happened next. Satan visited Eve in the garden as a serpent and whispered sin into existence. No longer was the world what God created. Paradise was lost—but not forever. God immediately went to work to solve a problem he was not responsible for.

See, we get it wrong when we say the first sin was when Eve took a bite of the fruit and then handed it to Adam. The first sin was Adam and Eve questioning God—thinking they knew better than their Creator.

Genesis 3:1–6 tells the story:

The serpent said to the woman, "Did God really say, 'You must not eat fruit from any tree in the garden'?"

The woman said to the serpent, "We may eat fruit from the trees in the garden. But God did say, 'You must not eat the fruit from the tree in the middle of the garden. Do not even touch it. If you do, you will die.'"

"You will certainly not die," the serpent said to the woman. "God knows that when you eat fruit from that tree, you will know things you have never known before. Like God, you will be able to tell the difference between good and evil."

The woman saw that the tree's fruit was good to eat and pleasing to look at. She also saw that it would make a person wise. So she took some of the fruit and ate it. She also gave some to her husband, who was with her. And he ate it.

The first sin wasn't the physical act of biting into the fruit. It was questioning God—questioning God's plan, God's goodness. It was the desire to *be* godlike. To be in control. It was *these* desires that led to a sin-soaked world. And we all hate sin. We hate what it does to us and what it does to the people we love. We hate it when people die young. We hate it when marriages are ripped apart. We hate it when natural disasters kill thousands of innocent people. We hate the bad things that happen.

But let me ask you this: Is *our* questioning of God any different from Adam and Eve's? Is our desire to have things go the way we want any different from their desire to be godlike, to be in control? How are our actions any different from the very actions that opened the doors to sin in our world?

Phew. I don't know about you, but that thought convicts me thoroughly.

But I'm not gonna leave y'all hanging here, because God sure didn't. I can't imagine what he must have felt when he learned of Adam and Eve's betrayal.

Brad and I recently moved our family back to Texas from Oklahoma (more on this later). My parents, Ed and Lisa Young, are the pastors of Fellowship Church. Brad and I are both on staff at our main campus in Grapevine. That means my kids are at church a *lot*. If you are a pastor's kid or your kids are pastor's kids, you know what I'm talking about. They're at church so much, they think they own the place.

Anyway, I had walked out of work and was trying to wrestle the kids into the car—Sterling (who's currently four) and Jackson (who's currently one). If you've ever carried a one-year-old in a car seat carrier for any amount of distance, you understand the fire that was burning in my forearm and bicep. I told Sterling, "Ster, hold on to Mommy's leg while I buckle in your brother." This is not an unfamiliar command. I make her touch me in the parking lot until I can get her secure.

I had just heard the satisfying *click* of the car seat into the base when Sterling squealed. And *ran* across the parking lot.

I thought I was going to come unglued. "STERLING, NO!" I yelled.

She ran with reckless abandon toward my dad's car, which was pulling back into the parking lot.

In that moment, Sterling thought she knew better than I did. In her eyes, she was doing something that felt right— running toward her papa. But in reality, what she did was incredibly dangerous. Thank God the parking lot isn't busy during the weekday, but can you imagine if she did that on a Sunday? With people backing in and out and darting around?

I couldn't leave Bubba by himself, so I waited until my dad walked her back to me. "Sterling, we do *not run* in parking lots."

"But I saw Big E," she said, as if that were an excuse to play dodge-the-SUV with her *body*.

I felt all the emotions. Relief that she was OK. Rage that she disobeyed. Rattled by what *could have* happened. And dread that she may disobey again and the result will be different—worse. Much worse. I imagine that my reaction to Sterling's disobedience is a faded shadow of what God felt in the garden of Eden when he learned of Adam and Eve's disobedience. He didn't give them the *one* rule to restrict them. He gave it to them for the same reason we give our kids most of their rules—to protect them. To protect us.

Once Adam and Eve sinned, the consequences were unavoidable. But God was determined to rescue his children. Romans 8:3 says, "The written law was made weak by the power of sin. But God did what the written law could not do. He made his Son to be like those who live under the power of sin. God sent him to be an offering for sin. Jesus suffered God's judgment against our sin."

Through the life, death, and resurrection of Jesus, God created a road map back to perfect union with him—through our faith in his Son. That's the love our Father has for us! Unwavering, undeterred, and unaffected by our actions. He is constant; he is *good*.

We don't have a God problem. We have a sin problem. Yes, I can get really worked up when I try to understand LeeBeth's death through my own thinking, my own reasoning, my own logic. But when I take a step back and think about it through the truth of God's Word, I may not make *sense* of it, but I can make *peace* with it. Some days, at least.

Typically, when we struggle it's because we're wrestling with acceptance. We're given a circumstance we don't want, and we think, *God did not consult me on this matter, and I'd really like to speak with his manager.*

When we try to live within our own power, we see God as unfair. We begin to question him and wonder if he is really with us as Job did when he said, "Why have you made me your target?" (Job 7:20 NIV). Have you asked that of God? Why is this happening to *me*? Why *her*? Why *us*? It's human nature to ask these things. It's completely understandable. But it's also the same as thinking we can see the whole picture better than God can.

Eventually, even Job (who lost more than I have) was able to come to a point of acceptance: "To God belong wisdom and power; counsel and understanding are his" (12:13 NIV).

So what do we do? Just stop praying? Just stop trying? Check out of our lives and let God do whatever he's going to do, because he's going to do it anyway? No, of course not. I mean, trust me, I've been in that season of life, and it's no better than the struggle. In fact, it's worse. It's isolating and detaching, and that is not how we were designed to live.

My dad has this statue in his office. It's the faces of two men—Paul and Jesus. Jesus is holding the back of Paul's head with one hand, almost lovingly, while his other hand touches Paul's eyes. Paul's face looks strained—as if he is in pain or discomfort. Jesus's face is serene with an almost knowing look in his eyes. If you've cracked open the Bible, you know who Paul (formerly, Saul) is. Paul was one of the biggest persecutors of Jesus followers in the history of humankind. Literally, he hunted down people following Jesus and had them arrested—or worse. But Paul is also responsible for most of the writing found in the New Testament. He is credited largely with the establishment of the first church. And he led countless people to Christ.

How did this come about? What happened? Paul suffered.

Have you ever thought about that? That Paul's very first interaction with Jesus was one of suffering?

While traveling to Damascus on the search for more Jesus followers to imprison, "suddenly a light from heaven flashed around him. [Paul] fell to the ground. He heard a voice speak to him, 'Saul! Saul! Why are you opposing me?'" (Acts 9:3–4).

Paul's like, *Um. Who. The. Heck. Are. You?*

"'I am Jesus,' he replied. 'I am the one you are opposing'" (v. 5).

Then Paul opened his eyes, but he couldn't see. He had been struck blind. I'm not going to make light of the loss of vision, but can you imagine the loss of control Paul must have felt? He had lost the way he interpreted everything—his sight. If I wake up in the morning and don't have my glasses on or contacts in, I am a legitimate hazard to myself and others. And here's Paul, this big, important religious zealot, with no control over his surroundings.

Paul's story continues and he encounters a man named Ananias, a man God had sent (though Ananias was reluctant, which I get because Paul was a scary dude) to help Paul. Ananias prayed for Paul, and something like scales fell from his eyes, and he could see again. Paul gave his life to Christ and the rest is literal history. But it all started with suffering.

Maybe, just maybe, our suffering serves a similar purpose. Maybe suffering is something God uses to teach us, grow us, and help us.

Does he send us suffering? Does he allow our suffering? These are questions we're not going to grapple with in this book, mostly because I'm not God. Some days, I'd like to think I'd be a good God, but I'll be honest. I found my wedding rings in a bag of sour candy last week. No idea how they got in there. No one wants me to be ruler of the universe.

What we *are* going to unpack, however, is the usefulness of suffering. Of what it brings. Of the—dare I say?—*gifts* that come as a result.

As I write this, I'm having a crappy week. I miss my sister. Someone at church told me on Sunday: "You look just like her, like LeeBeth." I know people mean well when they make these kinds of comments, but they sort of drive the stake of grief just a little deeper into my heart. I don't want to look like LeeBeth. I want LeeBeth to look like LeeBeth. I want LeeBeth to be alive.

But she isn't. Instead, LeeBeth suffered. Instead, I'm suffering. Instead, my family is suffering.

Are you suffering right now, friend? Does your life resemble a battlefield? In the aftermath, when you look around you, do you see nothing but mess after mess?

Have you lost someone you love? Have you lost a baby before you even held her? Have you lost the hope of ever being married because the dating scene has left you bitter and hurt? Have you lost trust in your spouse because of their actions? Or have your own actions cost you more than you're willing to lose? Few things grate on the heart quite like self-inflicted suffering.

Have you lost your health? Have you lost your dream? Have you lost faith in someone you trusted or faith in the entire country?

Paul lost his vision.

I lost my sister.

But I know my God. And I know he is good. Because of that, I can be certain that he will not waste my suffering. He will not waste *any* suffering—including yours.

2

Isolation Station

Because of how I suffered for Christ, I'm glad that I am weak. I am glad in hard times. I am glad when people say mean things about me. I am glad when things are difficult. And I am glad when people make me suffer. When I am weak, I am strong.

2 Corinthians 12:10

Have y'all seen my husband? I mean, I don't really want to invite women to gawk at him, but he really is the most handsome man on the planet. He is! God was feeling extra generous the day he dreamed up Bradford Hughes. When I met Brad for the first time, I'm pretty sure I drooled. But, like, not obviously because I was playing it cool.

(Sidebar: If you've read my first book, *A Different Kind of Love Story*, you already know I Insta-stalked Brad and completely orchestrated our first run-in. So I was probably playing it very *not* cool, but he's too much of a gentleman to tell me that.)

The only problem was that I lived in Dallas and Brad lived in Kokomo, Indiana—a fourteen-hour drive away. But when I tell you sparks flew, it was like the Fourth of July up in that church office where we first met. Obviously, Brad had to return to Indiana, but I was determined to see him again. We talked *constantly* after he left. Like, high school–crush level, falling asleep on the phone together. It wasn't long before we'd set a date for our first official meetup (well, the first date he knew about in advance).

We both drove the seven or so hours toward each other, meeting in the city of Memphis, Tennessee. I knew I wanted to marry Brad after that. And I'm glad God agreed, otherwise God and I would have had to go back and forth a little over it. Anyway, the next day when it was time for us to part ways, we were so reluctant to return to our homes that we both left a lot later than we should have, considering the long drives ahead of us.

This was before the days of all the hands-free laws, so we kept each other company during the commute by—you guessed it!—more talking on the phone. Isn't it absurd how long you can talk to someone on the phone when you're falling in love? Now we're like:

"Hey, you're getting the kids today, right?"
"Right. Chick-fil-A for dinner?"
"Obviously."
"Polynesian sauce."
"Duh."
Click!

Back then, it felt as if we had all the time in the world. In fact, I got so caught up in our conversation that I didn't realize when my gas light came on. Not for many, many miles. Another thing I lost track of? The time. It was late, very late.

"Umm, Brad?" I said.

"Hmm?"

"I'm about to run out of gas."

"Where are you?"

Imagine for a moment the last place in the entire world you'd like to run out of gas. Or, even more accurate, think about horror movies in which the main character is driving down a lonely stretch of highway when all of a sudden, their car breaks down. You know, right before they get axed or scythed or whatever bloody end they meet? That place? That's where I was.

"Um, I don't know," I answered. "Somewhere in Arkansas?"

"Do you see an exit?" he asked.

"No, I see . . . I see . . ." I didn't finish the sentence because I saw absolutely nothing. Nothing and no one resembling life.

"Landra?" Brad asked. His voice sounded strained. He was probably thinking about how he was going to explain my kidnapping to my father. Because I was certain at that point that I was *not* getting out of the situation with my life.

I opened the Maps app on my phone and saw that I was about ten minutes away from an exit with a gas station. I told Brad.

"OK, stay on the phone with me until you get there," he said.

By then, my mind was playing all sorts of tricks on me. Every bend or bump in the interstate had me convinced my car was sputtering to a standstill. I was staring at the dash-board of my car with Herculean intensity, as if somehow my attention would fuel it the few miles left between itself and the nearest (functioning) gas station. Maybe that's why I didn't see it.

I was looking from my phone to the dashboard, to the road, to the phone, to the dashboard when, *Wham!* I side-swiped Bambi.

"Oh, CRAP!" I yelled, and then I dropped my phone. When I picked it back up, it was dead. (This is a true story, by the way. I couldn't make this up.)

Searching the darkness around me, I caught the blur of Bambi's white tail as she darted back into the tree line, ap-parently uninjured. As for my car? I had no idea what state it was in or if it could safely get me anywhere.

So I did what any of you would do in the situation. I lost my mind.

Please, Jesus, I prayed. *Just let me get to this gas station!*

I was shaking everywhere. Literally, I was so jittery I could hardly hang on to the steering wheel. I managed to plug my phone into the car charger, but for some reason, it was taking forever to turn back on. Because God loves me, I did man-age to remember the correct exit number. I pulled off and approached the gas station, trying to control my breathing and my sobs.

Hand on Bible, the gas station had flickering lights. It looked haunted. There wasn't another car in the lot, but it was my only hope.

Pay Inside, the note on the pump said.

This is it, I thought. *I just met my husband, and now I'm going to die.*

I walked inside, paid the very scary-looking man behind the counter, and finally filled up my car. All the while, Brad was panic calling my dead phone as "Oh crap" was the last thing he'd heard from me.

"LANDRA!" he yelled when I was able to get back on the road and charge my phone. I think the phone was already ringing by the time it turned on. "I was literally looking up your dad's contact information to call him."

"It's OK," I told him. "I hit a deer, couldn't get my phone to work, and was pretty sure I was going to wind up in tiny pieces, scattered down the interstate, but . . . I'm OK."

Can any of you relate to that feeling? The feeling of being completely and hopelessly alone? I mean, it doesn't get much more isolated than a place you've never been with zero resources and a banged-up car. But maybe you feel isolated in a different way.

Maybe all your friends are married or having babies, and you're not.

Maybe you've moved to a new place and haven't found community yet.

Maybe your relationship with your partner or spouse leaves you feeling lonely.

Maybe you feel disconnected from God, and you're not sure why.

Maybe a toxic family relationship has left you feeling misunderstood, hurt, and isolated.

Maybe you've recently graduated, gotten married, had a baby, or hit a milestone that has alienated you from your people.

Maybe you've got a secret or an addiction and feel like no one knows the real you.

Maybe you feel alone in the middle of a crowded Target with your phone about to vibrate out of your back pocket and a toddler hanging off your legs.

There's something so unnerving about isolation. In the moment, it can feel completely indefinite, vast, and unnavigable. It's like being stuck in the bottom of a cold, dark well with the stone walls inching closer and closer.

There's a reason the justice system uses solitary confinement as a punishment. It's absolute misery. And the results can be catastrophic, both physically and mentally. In fact, the American Psychological Association tells us there is evidence linking perceived social isolation with adverse health conditions such as

> depression, poor sleep quality, impaired executive function, accelerated cognitive decline, poor cardiovascular function and impaired immunity at every stage of life. In addition, a 2019 study led by Kassandra Alcaraz, PhD, MPH, a public health researcher with the American Cancer Society, analyzed data from more than 580,000 adults and found that social isolation increases the risk of premature death from every cause for every race.[1]

Obviously, long-term isolation is not good. We all probably knew that, but even *perceived* isolation can be harmful to our minds and bodies and souls. In some cases, isolation can lead to premature death. And death to our joy, death to our peace, death to our ability to maintain a normal, stable life. Even death to our *health*. So if loneliness and isolation are so bad for us, why does God allow us to enter into these isolating situations?

I've experienced about every form of loneliness. When my dad was accused of stealing money from the church, a news story aired that I'm pretty sure everyone within a one-thousand-mile radius watched. The fallout was massive. People left black wreaths on our church doors. I don't know if they were trying to tell us they wanted us dead, but it was eerie and disturbing. I felt so lonely during that time that even my thoughts seemed to echo in the silence around me.

My eating disorder was isolating. When I kept it a secret, I felt like an imposter. When everyone knew, I felt like a failure whom no one trusted. Brad and I moved to Oklahoma in 2020 to start a sister campus of Fellowship Church. We had a toddler, I was pregnant, Brad was working all the time, and I knew no one, living far away from my family for the first real time in my life. My heart ached with loneliness.

Now losing my oldest sister has opened a door to a type of loneliness I can barely describe. My life has yet to feel whole again.

Yes, I've asked, *God, why? Why me? Why us? Why her? Why here?* I mean, wasn't curing loneliness God's first troubleshooting moment?

The LORD God said, "It is not good for the man to be alone. I will make a helper who is just right for him."

The LORD God had formed all the wild animals and all the birds in the sky. He had made all of them out of the ground. He brought them to the man to see what names he would give them. And the name the man gave each living creature became its name. So the man gave names to all the livestock, all the birds in the sky, and all the wild animals.

But Adam didn't find a helper that was just right for him. So the LORD God caused him to fall into a deep sleep. While the man was sleeping, the LORD God took out one of the man's ribs. Then the LORD God closed the opening in the man's side. Then the LORD God made a woman. (Gen. 2:18–22)

I imagine the world Adam saw was absolutely breathtaking. Pre-pollution, pre-industrialization, pre-us. I think of every scene from The Lord of the Rings movies. And all the animals, all the streams, all the flowers were not enough for Adam. So God created another person. See, we've needed other people since the actual beginning of time.

If isolation is so bad for us, and God obviously wants us to have other people in our lives, then *why* do so many of us suffer from the messy feelings of loneliness? To understand that answer, we first have to define the varying shades of "lonely" we may experience.

Reactive Isolation

Reactive isolation happens when circumstances out of our control take us away from people we love and care about. A new job means a new city, state, or country. Kids move out of the house and go to college. A spouse decides to leave. Someone close to you dies. This type of loneliness, while incredibly painful, is somewhat understandable. These situations are intrinsic to life. Things change. People change. We don't live on this earth forever.

But sometimes, reactive isolation makes us question God more than any of the others. Because it all seems subjective, right? Why did their relationship work, but mine didn't? Why did they get to have their own kids, but we're experiencing infertility? Why did cancer enter our family? Why did addiction?

Self-Inflicted Isolation

Self-inflicted isolation occurs when either we choose to separate ourselves from others or they choose to separate from us based on our actions. Take LeeBeth, for example.

I believe loneliness was at the root of LeeBeth's drinking. She was the oldest of four children, all of whom she watched grow up, meet people, fall in love, get married, and have children (well, two of us currently have kids).

Now think about this: LeeBeth's biggest dream and ultimate goal in life was to be a wife and mother. And she sat through engagement parties, bridal showers, weddings, baby showers, kids' birthday parties. All the while, she had to be thinking, *God, when is it my turn?* My entire body just throbs with pain when I think about what that must have felt like for her. And if that's you, I am so sorry. It's not fair.

LeeBeth withdrew from anyone who cared about her when she was drinking (self-inflicted isolation). One day, when my mom couldn't get in touch with her, she called my dad. When *neither* of them could get ahold of her, they called a family friend who lived close to LeeBeth.

"Can you go knock on LeeBeth's door? We're worried."

So our family friend went to LeeBeth's, but her door was locked and she wasn't answering it. He walked around the house and was able to see through one of the windows. I won't share every detail of my sister's struggle because I want to be respectful. But what he saw through the window was highly alarming. Enough so that my dad asked him to force his way into the house to get to her.

That night, LeeBeth was checked in to a substance abuse rehabilitation center. When she got out, I was so excited to connect with her. I know what that feels like—being checked in to a facility and knowing that your secret is out. I went to more than one facility in dealing with my eating disorder, and I looked forward to supporting my sister in her recovery.

Prior to LeeBeth going to rehab, our relationship had been extremely surface level. She'd already detached herself from our family, declining invitations, canceling last minute, or just not showing up. She was so secretive about her loneliness. I hate to say it, but she was often dishonest because of her addiction. She created distance to keep that secret safe.

She finally got back from rehab and insisted on my parents picking her up from the airport. Then she moved in with them for a while. Let's be honest—they wanted and needed to watch her. Those first few weeks out of treatment are so . . . weird. You're embarrassed, you're excited, you're scared of yourself, you're proud of yourself. LeeBeth did well that summer. She even wrote me a letter to apologize for the nasty things she'd said and for being a flake. She said she wanted to reconcile our relationship.

I'd like to say LeeBeth and I enjoyed that last year of her life by developing a genuine relationship, but we didn't. As soon as she left my parents' house, I suspect she relapsed because she went back to her old patterns—being late or not being there at all. She isolated.

Secrets do that though. Secrets always, always isolate. Even if we think we've got our secret addiction under control, its insidious nature will always draw us back into it.

I know this from my own experience with secrets. If you haven't read my first book, I'll give you a snapshot of just how life-threatening my secrets got.

When I was a teenager, I developed a severe eating disorder. I was stuck in a cycle of starvation, binge eating, and purging that I couldn't stop. I even had a doctor tell me I would die if I didn't get it under control. But her warning wasn't enough. I kept returning to my secret addiction like a woman returning to an abusive relationship. I knew it was hurting me, but I felt as if I couldn't stop.

Secrets force us to self-isolate. The secret itself becomes more important to us—safer to us—than the actual people who love us. We decide that we can't let those people in anymore because they may discover our secret. I was willing to make myself physically ill and self-isolated in order to conceal my secret. And for years, that's how I lived my life.

Secrets can be thrilling. They're like a piece of the universe that only belongs to us. The thing is when the secrets are *our* secrets, they don't really feel as if they're hurting anyone. I'm sure that's what LeeBeth assumed. I did too. Sure, there may be some recognition on our parts that what we're doing could become potentially harmful, but we continue to justify our hidden actions, unwilling to relinquish our perceived control of our secrets.

But maybe it isn't a secret you're keeping. Maybe it's anger, bitterness, jealousy, unforgiveness, or hurt. You can't get over something that's happened to you, so you isolate. You withdraw. Or maybe your emotions have taken control of how you talk to or treat people. Maybe you push people away, or maybe they run away because you're a prickly person to love. It's all self-inflicted isolation.

Chronic Isolation

If reactive isolation is painful, chronic isolation is torturous. Chronic isolation or loneliness happens for no discernible reason at all. That example of a person who feels alone in a crowded Target? That's who I'm talking about. Someone who feels completely isolated with their spouse sitting beside them and their kids running all around them. This may be the most baffling type of isolation there is.

Typically, chronic loneliness is a result of dissatisfaction with your life. Maybe you thought your marriage was going to "fix" something that felt broken. Or you thought your job, your kids, or your friends were the answer to that stirring in your heart for something *more*. Maybe you're just straight-up bored with life. You think, *Is this it? Is this what it's going to be like . . . forever?*

This type of isolation is maddening because it's a little more challenging to pinpoint its source.

There's a woman in the Bible we can all probably relate to, at least in part. She isn't named in the story but is instead referred to as the woman with "a sickness that made her bleed." Jesus had just come ashore. People were gathering around him and following him wherever he went, asking him to heal or help their loved one in need. In that crowd of people was a woman—the woman with the issue of blood. We read her story in Mark 5:25–34:

> A woman was there who had a sickness that made her bleed. It had lasted for 12 years. She had suffered a great deal, even though she had gone to many doctors. She had spent all the money she had. But she was getting worse, not better. Then she heard about Jesus. She came up behind him in the

crowd and touched his clothes. She thought, "I just need to touch his clothes. Then I will be healed." Right away her bleeding stopped. She felt in her body that her suffering was over.

At once Jesus knew that power had gone out from him. He turned around in the crowd. He asked, "Who touched my clothes?"

"You see the people," his disciples answered. "They are crowding against you. And you still ask, 'Who touched me?'"

But Jesus kept looking around. He wanted to see who had touched him. Then the woman came and fell at his feet. She knew what had happened to her. She was shaking with fear. But she told him the whole truth. He said to her, "Dear woman, your faith has healed you. Go in peace. You are free from your suffering."

This woman's condition lasted for twelve years. *Twelve* years. I've had two children and am pregnant with my third. I've experienced blood and bleeding. *But for twelve years?* Even Jesus calls her struggle *suffering.*

According to Jewish law, this woman would have been ostracized from her entire community—even from her friends and family. If someone touched her, even accidentally, they, too, would have been considered unclean. How do you think it would feel to go over a decade without a hug or a hand squeeze? Without so much as a gentle hand on your shoulder?

This woman had to have been despairingly lonely, desperate to be healed. And yet, somehow, despite all she'd gone through, she scraped together the courage to reach out to Jesus.

This woman is a flipping hero, in my opinion. Twelve years of being a social pariah and she still let her faith be bigger than her fear.

After we've experienced a season of isolation, it can be hard to reengage in relationship—especially with God. But reaching out is *exactly* what stands between us and freedom from our suffering. Maybe for you, that's reaching out to a therapist, counselor, or pastor. Maybe it's reaching out to the sister you're not speaking to or the friend you hurt. Maybe it's coming humbly to your spouse or your children and offering an apology first, even though you may think you're the one who deserves the "I'm sorry."

Or maybe . . . maybe you need to reach out to God. Maybe you need to get on your knees before the one who created you—the one who knows things about you that *you* don't even know. Maybe that's the value in the struggle of loneliness and isolation—the overwhelming realization of just how very much we need a savior.

But if you want a list, here are two strategic ways God leverages our seasons of isolation:

- Loneliness is character building.
- Loneliness brings us closer to God.

Paul knew about the potential for our weaknesses to turn into our strengths. In 2 Corinthians 12:10, he says, "Because of how I suffered for Christ, I'm glad that I am weak. I am glad in hard times. I am glad when people say mean things about me. I am glad when things are difficult. And I am glad when people make me suffer. When I am weak, I am strong."

During our times of suffering our commitment and integrity are tested. When Brad and I were isolated in Oklahoma, we were *for sure* tested. I won't say I scored perfectly on every test, but I will say I returned to Dallas a different Landra. I was stronger, more direct, and had more clarity for what I wanted in life. Brad and I were closer, and God and I were closer.

Our loneliness can bring us closer to God—if we let it. But God needs an "in" with us. Our world continues to reach new heights of busyness. You've been hearing that for years, and we still get busier and busier. The pandemic may have momentarily slowed us down in some ways, but in others it gave us new distractions to divide our attention.

Sometimes God has to remove those distractions completely in order to get our undivided attention. I think about Sterling. If her favorite show is on or if she's on a playdate with a friend, I have no chance of communicating with that girl. But if I turn off the iPad or walk her into a room by herself, she listens. Ster certainly isn't happy about it, but sometimes I have to isolate her to get her to listen.

Jesus got this. In Luke 5:16 we read, "But Jesus often withdrew to lonely places and prayed" (NIV). In fact, we're told many times throughout the Gospels that Jesus's destination for prayer was a "lonely" place of isolation.

In the same way, God draws us away to our "lonely" place because he wants more time with us.[2] Because without all the noise, we can hear him better. Because he wants to hang out with us. Because he wants us to know him better and to grow in discernment. Because he knows what's ahead and wants to prepare us for it.

Maybe loneliness isn't God taking something away from us but giving us something we don't even know we need.

So what does this look like in everyday life? Will our loneliness just go away because we know God wants to leverage it for good? Of course not. That would defeat the purpose of the season. But there are some simple things we can do to avoid needless isolation.

For one, stop doing anything that constantly leaves you lonely. Just stop. Someone asked me once, "Landra, how did you stop bingeing and purging? I've been to therapy. I've been to treatment. I've got a counselor and support groups, but I just can't stop."

Here's what I said: "You just stop."

Aren't you glad you're reading a book written by someone of such deep and meaningful wisdom? But seriously—just stop doing things that make you lonely. Take social media, for instance. Social media does us no favors in our loneliness. For a technology meant to connect us, it often makes us feel super disconnected. If we think feeling left out ended with middle school slumber parties, we'd be wrong. To be honest, social media can make me feel left out rather quickly. In fact, I'm on a break from the 'Gram right now.

If something hurts you or isolates you, be disciplined enough—love *yourself* enough—to just stop. Can't stop on your own? Ask for help. If you're choosing isolation, you're choosing death in areas of your life and health that are not worth compromising.

What about those of you who are lonely due to no fault of your own? Be like the woman with the issue of blood. Reach out—today. Reach out to a friend, a counselor—or even anonymously to an online support group. It takes courage, yes. But your joy, peace, and freedom can and will be restored.

God doesn't always want something *from* you—often, he wants something *for* you. When you find yourself at an "isolation station," ask yourself, *What could God's good purpose be for me here?*

Remember, you are not alone. Regardless of how desolate the landscape around you looks, God is with you.

3

What a Girl Wants

Brothers and sisters, God has shown you his mercy. So I am asking you to offer up your bodies to him while you are still alive. Your bodies are a holy sacrifice that is pleasing to God. When you offer your bodies to God, you are worshiping him in the right way.

Romans 12:1

Back to the *Bachelor* franchise. Y'all, I don't even know where to begin. I feel like I need therapy over this. I think we can all agree on one point—*The Bachelor* and *The Bachelorette* are just not what they used to be. The happy ending isn't there anymore. In fact, the happy ending isn't even the *point* anymore. It's all about the drama now. It's all about the twist, the shocker, the cliff-hanger. But it's all so painfully staged—scripted, almost.

It's like going to a puppet show, right? You know there are puppet masters making the characters talk and walk, but they're hidden. But when I watch an episode in the *Bachelor* franchise now, it's like I can see the puppet strings and the hands of the producers dipping onto the screen, orchestrating bombshell after bombshell.

Obviously, I'm still going to watch. Let's not get crazy—I still want to know what happens. But I won't enjoy it. Much. It makes me sad because, back in the Sean and Catherine days, I thought the show was the best thing ever. Like, in the world.

If you have no idea what I'm talking about, then good for you. You're probably a more disciplined person than I am, someone who makes wholesome entertainment choices. Trash TV? It's my favorite vice. I want my nonsense show to go back to the way it was before—when it was about finding true love and connection. But I realize that I'm not going to get my way, not by a long shot.

Isn't that how we're wired as humans? To want what we want. We don't think about it, but our desires control a big part of our lives. Do we want to work out? Do we want to go to church? Do we want to be social? Do we want to eat healthy? *Do we want to ruin a perfectly good television show?*

We're driven by our want-tos. You might say, "Landra, I spend my entire day doing stuff I don't want to do." And on the surface, that might be true. But if you look deeper, you'll see that our don't-want-tos get overridden by a less obvious but more pressing want-to. Let me give you some examples. You don't want to work out, but you want to be in shape. So you work out. You don't want to go to church, but you want your kids to. So you go to church. You don't want to be social, but you want friends. So you go out. You don't want to eat healthy, but you want to fit into your clothes. So you eat a salad.

You don't want to destroy the sanctity and tradition of a long-standing TV show that many people are emotionally invested in, but you want to make money. *So you destroy it with artificial drama.*

See? Our want-tos are a powerful driving force in our lives. But what happens when our want-tos are broken? When our want-tos are the opposite of God's plan for us? We know it's possible. Even Paul said, "I don't do the good things I want to do. I keep on doing the evil things I don't want to do" (Rom. 7:19).

That verse honestly makes me laugh a little. I'm like, "OK, postsalvation Paul. What'd you do that was so evil? Interrupt your three-hour morning prayer with a potty break?" I'm sure Paul's threshold for "evil" was very different from yours and mine.

To keep our want-tos under control, there must be intentionality in how much power we give to our own desires. Our biggest want-to—the want-to that overrides all others—has to be finding peace with God's want-to.

And that takes *surrender.*

What does it look like to surrender? Well, I wish it were as easy as giving in to sleep when you're exhausted, but that's not always the case. Surrender is to cease resistance, yield control, and give yourself up to the power of another. To surrender is to lay down what is most precious to you—your heart's desire—and say to God, "It's yours. If you give it back to me, I will praise you. If you don't give it back to me, I will still praise you."

If you've ever been around a toddler who is fighting sleep, you know what the *opposite* of surrender looks like. Jackson is just getting to the age when he fights his first nap. He sings to himself to stay awake. Sings, then cries. Talks, sings, cries. Then, cries, cries, cries. He's miserable. I can try driving him around in the car, I can rock him, I can leave him in a cool, dark room with soothing music. But his desire to stay awake, his want-to, is bigger than his want-to to feel better. I think, *What wouldn't I give for someone to be begging me to take a nap?* But he fights it. Until finally, he surrenders to what's best for him. He sleeps, he wakes up, and he's happier. And you better believe Mama's happier too.

I wonder how often we act like toddlers fighting sleep when we won't surrender to what's best for us. If I, as Jackson's earthly parent, know what's best for him, how much more does our omniscient God know what's best for us? But in our own minds, our desire to get our way seems so logical. To us, our desire is what we *need* and what we *deserve*. And God is shaking his head, driving us around in the metaphorical car of life, glancing at us in the rearview mirror, just begging us to surrender. To do what's ultimately best for everyone.

Here's a question to think about: Where do our desires come from? LeeBeth wanted what many women want: a loving relationship, marriage, and children. It wasn't unreasonable. And those had to be God-given desires, right? God created us to have dreams. We were created by a passionate God to be a passionate people. So why would God give us a want-to, then not allow us to possess it?

We have to reframe what surrender means to us. When we fail to surrender, it's the same as saying we are in control.

Some of the most difficult tensions we encounter as Christians (and humans) involve the desire to control. To be in charge. To be calling the shots. Not just in our own lives but also in the lives of the people around us. I remember when my brother, EJ, was dating, and I said to him, "If you would just give me your phone and let me do the texting, I will get you any girl you want." As if to say, just give me control. (By the way, EJ did *not* need my help. He married the most amazing and beautiful woman because he's completely charming all on his own. I'm just *that* sister.)

Have you ever heard of anything so arrogant in your life? Desiring control doesn't feel that way when we're hurting or frustrated because we're not getting what we want, but it's actually beyond hubristic. Besides, you can't surrender what doesn't actually belong to you. In the case of control, surrendering simply means acknowledging what is already true—that God is the master of the universe and his will reigns supreme.

If you're familiar with the recovery process at all, you've heard of twelve-step programs. The twelve steps were created in 1946 by the founders of Alcoholics Anonymous as guidelines to overcome an addiction to alcohol. Now these steps are applied in most recovery programs. If we were to get gut-level honest with ourselves, we'd say our want-to for control can become obsessive—much like an addiction. Want to know what the first step to recovery is? *We admitted we were powerless over [our problems].*[1]

See, surrender isn't really about giving up. It's about admitting what has always been true. As finite beings, we're powerless over pretty much everything. Everything, that is, besides our own thoughts, words, and actions—and our own *reactions* when we don't get our way. Step two is *We came to believe that a Power greater than ourselves could restore us to sanity.*[2] Isn't it illogical to assume that we know what's best for ourselves and others? That we know better than the God who knows all? That we should be in control?

When I think of people in the Bible who got this *wrong*, the first person who comes to mind is King Nebuchadnezzar. I mean, even his name sounds patronizing, and it kind of is. It means "may Nebo protect the crown." If you don't think there's significance in names, this story may change your mind.

King Nebuchadnezzar was the king of Babylonia. He had the most influential and longest reign of the Babylonian Empire, sitting on the throne from 605 to 562 BC. Nebuchadnezzar started off as a powerful and formidable leader. He greatly expanded the Babylonian Empire, rebuilt and revitalized his hometown and the capital city, Babylon, and is even credited with the architectural achievement of the Hanging Gardens—one of the seven wonders of the ancient world.

But as brilliant a strategist as he was, Nebuchadnezzar was just as complicated. And there is no shortage of stories in the Bible where his narcissism was on full display.

Nebuchadnezzar was a pretty ruthless military tactician who used whatever means necessary to increase the boundaries of his kingdom, destroying cities and plundering temples as he pleased (Dan. 1:1–2). It's said that he prayed to Marduk, the patron god of Babylon, to "have no opponent from horizon to sky."[3] By brute force, Nebuchadnezzar realized his own prayer, even if only for a period of time.

There was also that one time when he summoned a group of "wise" men to come interpret his dreams. His reaction to their inability to meet his demands is a perfect demonstration of his toddler-like control over his emotions. "He ordered that all the wise men in Babylon be put to death" (Dan. 2:12). Oh, and by the way, Nebuchadnezzar hadn't even bothered to describe the dream that had troubled him before ordering the slaughter of an entire group of people—some who weren't even there when he insisted on the interpretation.

Yet there are moments when you think Nebuchadnezzar might *get it*. Might *get God*. It wasn't that he didn't *want* the truth. Because he did. He sought out interpretations to dreams that disturbed him because those dreams seemed to contain a deeper meaning. And sure, he was able to get glimpses of the truth. Daniel was able to interpret the dream accurately, awing Nebuchadnezzar, who admitted, "I'm sure your God is the greatest God of all. He is the Lord of kings. He explains mysteries" (Dan. 2:47). But just one chapter later, he builds a golden statue and demands that everyone—including three Israelites named Shadrach, Meshach, and Abednego—bow down to the statue or be burned to a crisp for refusing to worship it. Do you think this statue was very sacred to the king? That it held some great, religious meaning to him? No. But Nebuchadnezzar demanded his sovereignty of rule, even over the sovereignty of the God he'd just been praising a chapter before.[4]

Nebuchadnezzar wanted to acknowledge God's supremacy only when it seemed as if God were giving him what he wanted. But if circumstances didn't line up with his want-to, Nebuchadnezzar took matters into his own hands—his violent, mercurial hands. Much like the meaning of his name, if something didn't further his crown, his rule, or his way, Nebuchadnezzar reclaimed control for himself. In Daniel 3–4, God continued to show the king that, in fact, it is God who is most powerful.

In Daniel 3:28–29, after Shadrach, Meshach, and Abednego are left untouched by the fiery furnace, Nebuchadnezzar declares:

> May the God of Shadrach, Meshach and Abednego be praised! He has sent his angel and saved his servants. They trusted in him. They refused to obey my command. They were willing to give up their lives. They would rather die than serve or worship any god except their own God. No other god can save people this way. So I'm giving an order about the God of Shadrach, Meshach and Abednego. No one may say anything against him. That's true no matter what language they speak. If they say anything against him, they'll be cut to pieces. And their houses will be turned into piles of trash.

Then, again *in the very next chapter*, Nebuchadnezzar is walking on the roof of his palace in Babylon, taking in the view. And he says, "Isn't this the great Babylon I have built as a place for my royal palace? I used my mighty power to build it. It shows how glorious my majesty is" (4:30).

King Nebuchadnezzar had a short memory. He looked at his successes and began to claim the credit for himself. He lost the humility of remembering that God rules and gives power and success "to anyone he wants" (v. 32).

See? The story of our lives is written according to what *God* wants. Not what we want. Not what we think we deserve. Not even what we've done because it's not us doing the "done." It's God *through* us.

Nebuchadnezzar wanted all the control and all the credit. Instead, he entered into a seven-year period of insanity. He was driven away from his people and became a shaggy, dirty vagrant. For *seven years* he grazed aimlessly with the cattle in the fields until he acknowledged what was always true—God is in control.

So what does his story have to do with us? Well, I think a lot. I think many of us have the tendency to believe God is good when our want-to is being met. When things are going our way. When we feel a false sense of control. But as soon as that's not the case? We're living within our power again. We're questioning God. Sometimes, we're even denying him.

LeeBeth never denied God. But I think instead of surrendering to him, she turned to alcohol to numb the pain. I've done this in my own life in different degrees. And maybe you've done it too. Maybe you've turned to alcohol or drugs to help you cope. Or maybe you've turned to receiving attention from men to temporarily ease the ache. Maybe you've become incredibly religious, and you work tirelessly to prove how very unaffected you are by the void in your soul. Or maybe you work tirelessly to *earn* what you want.

The truth is that none of those things will satisfy. They're not the things you really want for yourself, and they're certainly not the things God wants for you.

The Bible's book of wisdom, Proverbs, tells us that "a broken spirit dries you up" (17:22). The reality is that sometimes not getting what we want *hurts*. It creates a gaping wound inside us that we can't seem to mend. We feel empty, dried up, and dead inside.

What can we do about it? We can bring it to God. He does care about what we want. In John 1, John the Baptist is hanging out with two of his disciples. He sees Jesus and kind of elbows his friends and whispers, "Hey, that's him. That's the Messiah—the one I've been telling you about. He's greater than I am because he came after me but has existed since the beginning of time." (That's the Landra Young translation, by the way.) So the two disciples casually follow Jesus. I imagine them trying to play it cool but being in complete awe of the Son of God.

Because Jesus is Jesus (and these guys probably weren't *nearly* as low-key as they thought they were), he turned around to the two men and said, "What do you want?" (v. 38). Those are his first words in the Gospel of John. *What do you want?*

He asks you the same thing. What do you want right now?

A house?

A job?

A husband?

A healing?

A baby?

An answer?

A purpose?

God wants us to surrender those want-tos. He wants us to come to him, willing to give them up if it be his will. He wants us to trust his judgment, to have faith that he is working on our behalf in his own time.

Romans 12:1 says, "Brothers and sisters, God has shown you his mercy. So I am asking you to offer up your bodies to him while you are still alive. Your bodies are a holy sacrifice that is pleasing to God. When you offer your bodies to God, you are worshiping him in the right way."

Surrender is an act of worship. It's a holy sacrifice. It's a denial of oneself and a reliance on the Father. And surrender can be beautiful.

I'm not really a military buff. OK, let me rephrase. I am not *at all* a military buff. But I do remember in high school learning about the surrender of Japan to the United States in 1945 to end World War II. It stood out to me because there was a surrender ceremony held to commemorate the occasion, and I thought, *What? A ceremony? Did they hire a surrender-ceremony planner? Whose job was that?* I also remember the words the Allies used that prompted Japan's concession—they demanded *unconditional surrender.*

God is certainly not our enemy; he is our loving Father. But he wants the same from us—unconditional surrender. He knows what the Allied forces knew—that partial surrender isn't surrender at all. Partial surrender is like partial commitment. Like telling your spouse you'll be faithful six out of seven days a week. Unconditional surrender to God means that when we accept Jesus as our Savior, we hand over every aspect of our lives to him. We are not meant to keep certain parts back—especially the parts that mean the most to us—but to surrender our *entire* lives to him, every detail, in an act of obedience and complete trust.

But that's a lot easier said than done, isn't it? To relinquish the key to every room in our house? The thing is, I think most of us *want* to surrender to God. And we probably aren't even cognizant of it when we're not surrendering. While we want to be in control because that feels safe, it's also so much pressure. The weight of being in control is heavy and cumbersome.

The question is, How do we surrender control? When we're struggling with a "no" or "not yet" from God, how do we change what our heart wants? How do we fix our want-to? How do we surrender to God?

The first step is the first step in solving any problem—admitting that there is a problem. Acknowledge to yourself and to God that there are certain areas in your life that you aren't fully surrendering to him. Spoiler alert! He already knows. Maybe you already know too, but if you don't, how can you identify these areas? Any thing, person, or circumstance that you obsess over, overthink, or carry anxiety about you're probably not surrendering to God.

When we're trying to let go, when we're trying to give God our itineraries, the second step is to spend time in prayer. First John 5:14–15 says, "Here is what we can be sure of when we come to God in prayer. If we ask anything in keeping with what he wants, he hears us. If we know that God hears what we ask for, we know that we have it."

Prayer shifts our perspective. It takes a "me" problem and brings it into a "we" context. When we ask "in keeping with what he wants," we're already loosening the reins of the hold on our lives. Through prayer, we have access to the only one who can answer our questions. We are able to find out what God wants us to do in certain situations or what God is saying about specific needs. Prayer invites God in. It allows us to verbalize to God that we are laying down our plans, that we want to rely on him, and that our biggest want-to is to seek his will.

Another step toward surrender is to get into his Word. The Bible is the living, breathing Word of God, which makes it another direct line to him, his character, and his will. It's also an opportunity to ask ourselves some tough questions: Do our want-tos line up with who God is and what he says? Is there a situation in the Bible that translates into our situations? I can promise you there is nothing new under the sun. Many of the issues we deal with today have been around since the beginning of time. What verses or stories can we hold on to from his Word that can bolster our faith while we're waiting for God to act?

When I read the Bible, one thing I try to do is to replace my words with God's words. I'm sure you've read or heard of the many studies that stress the effect words have on our lives. It might be hard to believe that the little things we say to ourselves (or about ourselves) can actually steer the direction of our lives, but they can and they do. What we say (in our heads or out loud) eventually becomes what we believe. What we believe eventually becomes what we do.

In Mark 11:23, we read about the kind of belief we're capable of through Christ: "What I'm about to tell you is true. Suppose someone says to this mountain, 'Go and throw yourself into the sea.' They must not doubt in their heart. They must believe that what they say will happen. Then it will be done for them."

What if we lived like that were true? But if it's in the Bible, and we believe God's Word is infallible, then *isn't it true*?

All that's required to enjoy a mountain-throwing level of belief is *faith*. Let's start speaking God's Word into our struggles. Instead of blaming him or withdrawing from him, let's *partner* with him by believing what his Word says.

The next step, and maybe even the hardest, is to actually let go. John 15:5–8 tells us:

> I am the vine. You are the branches. If you remain joined to me, and I to you, you will bear a lot of fruit. You can't do anything without me. If you don't remain joined to me, you are like a branch that is thrown away and dries up. Branches like those are picked up. They are thrown into the fire and burned. If you remain joined to me and my words remain in you, ask for anything you wish. And it will be done for you. When you bear a lot of fruit, it brings glory to my Father. It shows that you are my disciples.

One lesson to be learned from surrender is what needs to be removed from our lives. Have you ever seen a line of trees or group of bushes that have been pruned? They're ugly, sad looking. They don't even look alive. Stripping away our control, our want-to? The pruning of our souls is rarely a pretty process. Sometimes surrender requires us to give up parts of our lives that we're clinging to, maybe a relationship, a job, a habit, or an ideal.

One of the most difficult things to let go? Our expectations. We expect certain things out of life and from God, maybe because we've done the "right" things or because we're a "good" person. Or maybe because God's given our want-to to someone else, and we think we deserve it too. When that happens, we feel like crap. I call it an expectation hangover. I've walked around in that messy state so many times, just completely heartsick over not getting my want-to.

A story I find seriously bizarre and yet just as comforting is the one about the prophet Balaam and a talking donkey from the Old Testament. Haven't heard of it? I'm not surprised. It's a weird one.

Going against God's will, Balaam attempted to travel to Moab. Because God will strike you blind or throw you into a whale's belly to get you where he wants you, it should come as no surprise that he intervened here as well. God sent the angel of the Lord to draw a sword and oppose Balaam (Num. 22:21–23). I'm not sure about you, but the single last thing I want to see looming in front of me is a locked and loaded Gabriel.

The problem was, Balaam couldn't see the life-threatening danger ahead. Oh, but his donkey could. Like you and I would do if we were the donkey, he tried everything he could to get Balaam's attention. He turned aside, then pressed Balaam's foot against a wall, and finally, bless him, he lay down in downright refusal to go any farther. I personally think that donkey deserved a treat. But ol' Balaam didn't get it. He kept getting angrier and angrier (vv. 23–27).

Here's what happened next:

> Then the LORD opened Balaam's eyes. He saw the angel of the LORD standing in the road. He saw that the angel was holding a sword. The angel was ready for battle. So Balaam bowed down. He fell with his face to the ground.
>
> The angel of the LORD spoke to him. He asked him, "Why have you hit your donkey three times? I have come here to oppose you. What you are doing is foolish. The donkey saw me. It turned away from me three times. Suppose it had not turned away. Then I would certainly have killed you by now. But I would have spared the donkey."

Balaam said to the angel of the LORD, "I have sinned. I didn't realize you were standing in the road to oppose me. Tell me whether you are pleased with me. If you aren't, I'll go back." (vv. 31–34)

I have felt so confident on the paths my want-tos led me. I've even felt "called" to places by my want-tos, only to find my way cut short by immovable obstacles time and again. While I've never had a donkey lay down in the street, I have had my car break down (literally and metaphorically). These roadblocks along our most determined paths can provoke our impatience, anger, and embarrassment.

But could it be that our momentary disappointment and discomfort are, in fact, small inconveniences compared to the danger ahead that we can't see if we were given our want-tos? And could it be possible that if our eyes were fully opened to see what God sees, we might thank him for what feels today like a painful setback but is actually a merciful refusal for our own good?

I thank God for all the times he didn't give me what I wanted for my own protection. I thank God that my disappointment is the small price I paid for his divine intervention.

Let me just say this: God's comfortable with our disappointment. In fact, he wants us to talk to him about it. He wants to become our biggest want-to, and there are no lengths he won't go to in order to draw us closer to him and closer to his perfect will and way and want-to for our lives.

What are your biggest want-tos? Are you bringing those desires before God? If you haven't surrendered an area of your life or your heart to God, are you willing to try? Yes, giving up your dreams and hopes and wishes may be painful for a season, but God's Word promises his good purpose is still at work: "We know that in all things God works for the good of those who love him. He appointed them to be saved in keeping with his purpose" (Rom. 8:28).

4

Do I Smell Something Burning?

Are you tired? Worn out? Burned out on religion? Come to me. Get away with me and you'll recover your life. I'll show you how to take a real rest. Walk with me and work with me—watch how I do it. Learn the unforced rhythms of grace. I won't lay anything heavy or ill-fitting on you. Keep company with me and you'll learn to live freely and lightly.

Matthew 11:28–29 MSG

I set a girl's hair on fire once.

I mean, not on purpose. Y'all don't get crazy. It was the Christmas service at my church, and I was maybe ten or eleven years old. In keeping with the old-school tradition of holding candles with the little saucer-shaped paper at the bottom to catch the melting wax, our children's choir was singing carols for a packed-out audience.

If you know me, you know I have a tendency to space out from time to time. And this was one of those times. I don't remember specifically which glittery decoration or sparkly light had caught my eye, but I do remember that I was staring off into the distance, halfheartedly singing "Away in a Manger" and probably fantasizing about the Barbie Dreamhouse I wanted under the tree.

I was the first person to smell it. And if you've ever smelled burning hair, you know it's a stench from the pit of hell itself. I drew in a few, deep breaths and wondered, *Is someone's hair on fire?* This was about the same time that I realized I had leaned my brightly burning symbol of Christ's Christmas hope into the beautiful, curly hair of the girl in front of me.

I yanked back my candle and quickly blew out any lingering embers. Bless her heart, she didn't even realize what I'd done. And I never told her. Just continued right on singing like the preacher's kid that I am. I wish I could remember who my victim was so I could send her a hair salve or something. But, in my defense, who was the first choir director who decided it was safe to give a group of small kids candles and have them huddle together on a stage? I mean, we're talking about kids who aren't even allowed to use a toaster yet holding tiny flame sticks in close proximity to one another.

At any rate, that sweet girl's hair was straight up *burned*. Maybe you've burned something on your body before. I have a scar on my arm from when I was three years old and I touched a motorcycle engine that had just been turned off. I love cooking for my family, but I'm notorious for taste testing a little too soon. There may not be a single taste bud left on the tip of my tongue. Burns hurt, and half a million Americans find themselves in the ER every year from burn-related injuries.[1]

But I wonder how many of us each year experience another kind of burning? The burns that come from being too busy, too stretched, and too exhausted—burn*out*. I bet those numbers are significantly higher than half a million, especially for those of us who are parents with young kids or who are in ministry. (Oh, and by the way, if you're a Bible-believing Christian, you are in ministry.)

You've heard all the statistics, but just to give you an updated picture of what burnout looks like, according to LinkedIn's Glint platform, which surveyed more than 1.75 million working individuals, burnout has risen by 33 percent since the onset of the global pandemic.[2] Is it any wonder? We have been in the middle of the biggest social experiment of anyone's lifetime. We've all experienced a complete upheaval of our routines. Companies have been forced to throw out all work norms, while being confronted with the inevitable layoffs a shrinking budget demands. So we've switched from in-person meetings to impersonal Zoom calls, asked employees to operate outside their comfort zones, and taken on extra work, all while many of our kids were not in school, or if they were, it was in an unfamiliar, COVID-friendly environment and structure.

If we weren't burned out before, we sure were then.

If you're one of the magical unicorns out there who hasn't felt worn out by the events of the last few years, I bow my knee to you. It's been scary, and it's been tough. But that's life, right? A journey of the unknowns.

Let's first start by defining the topic at hand. Here are some signs that you're currently in a season of burnout:

- Overall feelings of disconnection
- Cynicism
- Emotionally distant
- Chronically stressed
- Drained
- Unable to cope
- Reduced performance

You can be burned out from just about anything that repeats itself. Parenting, a job, a marriage, a friendship, a phase of life. You can even get burned out on boredom—on the monotony that life can be reduced to under certain circumstances.

But the big burnouts, the burnouts that really hurt, are more than just general fatigue. I'm not talking about the kind of burnout that happens when you've binge-watched *Outer Banks* on Netflix for ten straight hours. (Ahem, not that I've done that.) Big burnouts are deeper—they can make our lives feel like anything but living. They can leave us feeling depressed and anxious, they can leave us sleepless and restless, and they can even lead to despair.

What about you? Are you burned out right now? Do you feel lonely but avoid connection? Do you feel tired but can't sleep? Do you feel anxious but can't pinpoint why? Do you feel as if you've lost your purpose? Your drive? Your motivation? Maybe you even feel like you've lost yourself.

That's burnout. Listen to what the speaker in Ecclesiastes 1:2–11 says:

> "Meaningless! Everything is meaningless!"
> says the Teacher.

"Everything is completely meaningless!
  Nothing has any meaning."

What do people get for all their work?
  Why do they work so hard on this earth?
People come and people go.
  But the earth remains forever.
The sun rises. Then it sets.
  And then it hurries back to where it rises.
The wind blows to the south.
  Then it turns to the north.
Around and around it goes.
  It always returns to where it started.
Every stream flows into the ocean.
  But the ocean never gets full.
The streams return
  to the place they came from.
All things are tiresome.
  They are more tiresome than anyone can say.
But our eyes never see enough of anything.
  Our ears never hear enough.
Everything that has ever been will come back again.
  Everything that has ever been done will be done
    again.
  Nothing is new on earth.
There isn't anything about which someone can say,
  "Look! Here's something new."
It was already here long ago.
  It was here before we were.
No one remembers the people of long ago.
  Even those who haven't been born yet won't be
    remembered
  by those who will be born after them.

I don't know about you, but I want to give this speaker a hug. Because you know what? I've been there. I think we've all been there. Maybe you're there right now—where everything just seems pointless, "meaningless." Nothing feels new anymore. Everything feels tired and overdone. Nothing I do makes a difference. Nothing anybody does makes a difference. Life is just one big loop of actions that amount to . . . you guessed it—nothing.

How do we handle these feelings of monotony, especially if feeling burned out has been around as long as humankind? And in a culture that is constantly applying vice-like pressure to do, be, and give *more*, is burnout simply unavoidable?

I believe the answer lies in one of my favorite sections of Scripture, Matthew 11:28–29. But first let's look at the context of this passage. Jesus is a total vibe. He's irritated. (I love reading verses that reveal how fully human Jesus was when he was on earth. That's right—Jesus got moody too.)

Jesus had just sent out the twelve disciples to preach and teach in various cities. Giving his team space to do their own thing, Jesus went on his own to Galilee. As soon as his feet hit the shoreline, a multitude gathered around him. Does any parent feel like that when walking into their house after being gone? As soon as you open the door, children come pouring out of every doorway and attach themselves to your hip?

Amid the chaos, John the Baptist's disciples arrived on the scene to deliver a message to Jesus from his imprisoned cousin. Herod Antipas, son of Herod the Great, had thrown John in the slammer because he preached against the king for stealing his brother's wife, which makes sense to us, right? Let me see somebody try to take Brad Hughes! They'll have more than an angry preacher on their hands. Can you imagine if everyone today who balked at a political leader's decision got put in jail? I'm pretty sure we'd all be wearing stripes at some point.

Back to the Bible story. John was in jail for no good reason, cutting short a powerful ministry. He did, however, get to introduce and baptize Jesus as the Messiah, a prophetic message that gave Jesus street cred when he began his own teaching. But despite all John knew and had seen himself, he still had a question for Jesus: "Are you the Messiah . . . ? Or should we keep looking for someone else?" (Matt. 11:3 NLT).

Have your kids or friends or employees or boss or co-worker ever asked you a question that made you want to wrap your hands around their throats? Now, I am not encouraging violence. In fact, no violence. That's an order. But sometimes people can question us in a way that provokes a dark place within us. After John baptized Jesus in the Jordan, the Bible tells us that the heavens opened up and the Spirit of God descended on him like a dove, and a voice said, "This is my Son, and I love him. I am very pleased with him" (Matt. 3:17).

And still, *John had questions about whether Jesus was God's Son?*

You want to know what's worse than feeling enraged to the point of assault? Numbness, no emotional response at all. Just dejectedness (like the speaker in Ecclesiastes 1). I imagine that's the point Jesus's flesh had been brought to: *What else do I have to do, people? I'm over here raising folks from the dead and healing others through the hem of my clothes, and you still question me?*

I guess John had some expectations, didn't he? That Jesus would have broken him out of prison already, that the cell walls would have crumbled and the chains would have snapped. But that hadn't happened. On the surface, John's question was logical.

Every king who came to the throne in Jerusalem was anointed and a messiah of sorts. Each of them knew that God was going to bring the golden age with his anointed one. And I believe that every king prior to Jesus wondered, *Is it going to be during my reign?* Then they'd sin, or there was a war, or some other catastrophe occurred that resulted in that king being denounced by a prophet.

For the Israelites, it was a lot of breath holding, then sighing in disappointment. After one king proved himself to be fallible, they'd immediately start looking for the next. And John, who at some point had been *convinced* that Jesus was the Messiah they'd all been waiting for, began to waver because his expectations had not been met.

Before you get mad at John, think through the messianic expectations of the people. Most expected a savior who would expel the Gentile oppressors from the land and establish this glittery rainbow kingdom of sunshine and sparkles. It actually took the resurrection and the coming of the Holy Spirit at Pentecost before Jesus's own disciples—his best friends—were able to piece it all together (though Jesus had explained the plan in detail about fifty-eleven times).

That's the thing about expectations, y'all. We get burned out when we work and work and work, expecting a certain outcome that never comes to pass. And we look back at all we've done, all we've invested, and we're like, *Why didn't that work out? Why didn't I get my outcome? Why doesn't life look the way I thought it would?* Our efforts seem meaningless. It's heart-wrenching. But one thing you can be sure of: every outcome is within the influence of God. We may not have gotten our way, but what if God got his?

Jesus, probably trying very hard not to snap at John's disciples, I imagine, responded to his cousin's messengers:

> Go back to John. Report to him what you hear and see. Blind people receive sight. Disabled people walk. Those who have skin diseases are made 'clean.' Deaf people hear. Those who are dead are raised to life. And the good news is preached to those who are poor. Blessed is anyone who does not give up their faith because of me. (Matt. 11:4–6)

That's an interesting way to end his reply, isn't it? "Blessed is anyone who does not give up their faith because of me." In other words, "I may not be what you expected, but I am the Messiah." John knew that. Deep down. We know it too. We cannot let our unmet expectations cause us to lose our faith. John didn't; he died a martyr's death.

When Jesus heard that his friend and relative had been killed, the Bible says he "withdrew by boat privately to a solitary place" (Matt. 14:13 NIV). Jesus had known that, despite John's unmet expectations, despite John's questions, his cousin had kept the faith.

After John's messengers left, Jesus turned to the crowd that had congregated around him. I imagine he was thinking, *If these people had just believed, John wouldn't be in jail, questioning me.* So Jesus asks sarcastically, "What did you expect when you went out to see [John the Baptist] in the wild? A weekend camper? Hardly. What then? A sheik in silk pajamas?" (Matt. 11:8–9 MSG).

Jesus was, in his own way, defending John. You see, Jesus is comfortable with our questions. When we're suffering, as John was, it's OK to bring that suffering to God. In fact, we should. He wants to remind us of all he's already done—of all we've already seen as proof that he is the sovereign king, our Savior, our Messiah.

Jesus goes on to say:

What can I compare today's people to? They are like children sitting in the markets and calling out to others. They say,

"We played the flute for you.
    But you didn't dance.
We sang a funeral song.
    But you didn't become sad."

When John came, he didn't eat or drink as you do. And people say, "He has a demon." But when the Son of Man came, he ate and drank as you do. And people say, "This fellow is always eating and drinking far too much. He's a friend of tax collectors and 'sinners.'" By wise actions wisdom is shown to be right. (vv. 16–19)

Jesus was annoyed. He compared the Israelites to kids in the street, complaining because no one would play their games with them. Jesus said that because John came to them neither eating nor drinking, they said he had a demon. At the same time, because Jesus did come to them eating and drinking, they said he was a sinner. Basically, Jesus was dealing with a group of people who could not be pleased.

Can you relate to Jesus? Is there someone in your life who is never happy? No matter what you do, it's not right or not good enough? A danged-if-you-do and danged-if-you-don't relationship or partnership? Just relationally messy people? Well, Jesus has been there. The people in his own hometown rejected him as the Messiah. Can you imagine how painful that must have been? After all the miracles they had witnessed him perform with their own eyes, can you imagine how frustrating?

How draining and exhausting it must have been for Jesus to continually reveal who he was to a group of people who behaved no better than street kids. Talk about feeling like everything you do is meaningless. Talk about being burned out.

Jesus was pushed to a breaking point. In the following verses, he unleashed his frustration on the cities in which he'd proven himself the most but who had believed the least:

Doom to you, Chorazin! Doom, Bethsaida! If Tyre and Sidon had seen half of the powerful miracles you have seen, they would have been on their knees in a minute. At Judgment Day they'll get off easy compared to you. And Capernaum! With all your peacock strutting, you are going to end up in the abyss. If the people of Sodom had had your chances, the city would still be around. At Judgment Day they'll get off easy compared to you. (vv. 21–24 MSG)

Have you ever been around someone who never gets mad, and then they do and totally lose their temper? They explode a vomit of stuffed-down verbal turmoil, and everybody else standing around them is thinking, *Umm, Kathy, maybe you need a Diet Coke and a candy bar? Because, girl, you are not yourself today.* It's hard not to laugh. It's always like, what? Did we all just see what happened there? I have no idea what the crowd's reaction was to Jesus's tirade, and I'm pretty sure it wasn't funny at all to them. But for some reason, I love it and sort of want to laugh. Capernaum with your peacock strutting—get it together!

Jesus was all business in that moment, but then something happened—some realization clicked inside of him, and he broke into prayer: "Thank you, Father, Lord of heaven and earth. You've concealed your ways from sophisticates and know-it-alls, but spelled them out clearly to ordinary people. Yes, Father, that's the way you like to work" (vv. 25–26 MSG).

God doesn't serve our expectations but his own. His ways don't always compute in our brains, because we're not God. God is God for a reason.

Jesus, as only Jesus could do, turned the situation on its head. His fully God side showed in what he said next:

Jesus resumed talking to the people, but now tenderly. "The Father has given me all these things to do and say. This is a unique Father-Son operation, coming out of Father and Son intimacies and knowledge. No one knows the Son the way the Father does, nor the Father the way the Son does. But I'm not keeping it to myself; I'm ready to go over it line by line with anyone willing to listen." (v. 27 MSG)

Have you ever been in the middle of a good old-fashioned meltdown and then realized something that cut off the words tumbling from your mouth? Been there. "STERLING, I SAID WHERE ARE YOUR SH—" Oh, yeah. I put her shoes in the closet while she was napping.

That is sort of what happened to Jesus. See, these people were worn out too. Worn out by the "religion" of the Pharisees and all their many additions to the law given to Moses. So many that the law itself had become impossible to keep. The Pharisees sort of legislated as they went. If they felt threatened in any way, they threw up another order against it. Again, today, we'd all be in jail. How burned out would you be if every other morning you woke up to a new rule? If each time you walked out the door, you wondered if you were breaking a new law without knowing it? How draining and defeating.

When I read this story, I'm struck by the different perspectives of all the people involved—John the Baptist, Jesus, and the Israelites. In their own way, they were all experiencing feelings of burnout. It makes me wonder who has been burned out around me that I haven't even considered because I was too busy thinking about myself.

If you're feeling burned out right now, take a beat. Think about it: Who else could also be going through the same season? Who else could also be burned out by the same situation you are but perhaps for different reasons?

Finally, Jesus, perhaps struck by empathy, issued an invitation to all those listening:

Are you tired? Worn out? Burned out on religion? Come to me. Get away with me and you'll recover your life. I'll show you how to take a real rest. Walk with me and work with me—watch how I do it. Learn the unforced rhythms of grace. I won't lay anything heavy or ill-fitting on you. Keep company with me and you'll learn to live freely and lightly. (28–30 MSG)

There it is—our solution to the burnout epidemic. *Are you tired? Worn out? Burned out?* Jesus says, *Come to me.*

Imagine that Jesus is asking you those three questions right now. What would your response be? If it's yes, he has already issued you an invitation to a life-recovery retreat. He knows what you're up against—the expectations you have for yourself and those that others have placed on you. He's felt the same pressure you feel. The pressure to be perfect. The pressure to perform. The pressure to prove.

All we have to do is wake up and check our phones to feel that very pressure. We open up our social media and it's as if the hand of culture reaches through the screen and bears down on us until we feel like we might suffocate. It's engrained into our society—this demand for our time, attention, and investment.

Before we even got home from the hospital after I had Sterling, I remember feeling that it was immediately and absolutely necessary to get off the baby weight, have her signed up for Mommy and Me classes, and have a fully funded college fund for her. But she was just a wiggly, teeny baby at this point. I started off parenting feeling as if I were already *behind*. So how much would it take to push me to burnout? A whisper!

According to a 2019 study by the Pew Research Center, "The share of moms who are working either full or part time in the United States has increased over the past half-century from 51% to 72%, and almost half of two-parent families now include two full-time working parents."[3] At the same time, the United States ranks dead last in government-mandated paid leave for new parents. Over in Estonia, they get *eighty-six* weeks.[4] Eighty-six! That sounds about right to me. Especially after our second baby, Jackson.

The competing voices are a reality we all have to confront. We have to work, and it has to be creative and invigorating and meaningful. But we also have to parent, and it has to be all-natural, organic, and wholesome. Oh, and you have to hold an iced latte in front of a beautifully painted brick background while you do all of this. We're not going to get away from the expectations around us. The people in the Bible couldn't, and we're not any better than John the Baptist. So let's just all accept that we can't either.

But what we *can* do is prepare for battle. We can arm up to defend ourselves against the siege of our minds. How do we do this? We rest. I know, I know. It sounds counterproductive. It sounds impossible, actually. You want me to rest? Trust me, I'd love to, but I've got a list. I've got people counting on me. I've got bills that have to be paid.

But that's not the kind of rest I'm suggesting, nor is it what I believe Jesus was recommending. Jesus was saying that coming to him is synonymous with resting. The cure to burnout? Come to Jesus. He makes everything sound so simple, doesn't he? Maybe it *is* that simple. When we make Jesus and his Holy Spirit the priority in our lives, doesn't it shrink everything else? Doesn't the greatness of who he is and what he has to offer diminish the demands of everyone and everything else?

The type of rest Jesus is talking about here is, in his words, "a real rest" (v. 29 MSG). What's a "real rest"? Here's a verse you may have heard: "But put God's kingdom first. Do what he wants you to do. Then all those things will also be given to you" (Matt. 6:33).

When our priority becomes coming to God first, acknowledging his will, his call, and his purpose, that's where our souls find peace. The problem is we're searching for answers in the world. And that's why we become so wounded, because the world was never meant to fulfill us.

We all have our reasons for not coming to Jesus first. Maybe we're ashamed. Maybe we're busy. Maybe we're angry at him. Maybe we're just going through the motions of coming to him. Coming to Jesus requires us to dig deep into our own humility. It requires us to acknowledge that we need him, not just with our words but with our actions too.

If the struggle of burnout teaches us anything, it teaches us that we can accomplish nothing on our own outside of the divine intervention of our heavenly Father.

The question is, How do we come to Jesus? We trust. We remember what he's done. We begin our day with him—not with our phones, not with our emails, not with our spouses even—but with him. Because when he's the foundation we're building on, life is just more stable. We trade in expectations for gratitude, we take the commandment of a sabbath seriously, and we stop at nothing to obey his call.

Burnout is our body's and our spirit's reminder that we were not created for this world. No, we were made for so much more. We were purposed to live big lives in submission to him, through him, and for him.

When we lay down our own wants, desires, dreams, wishes, work, kids, lives, and crosses, and simply and completely submit to Jesus, we actively demonstrate where our faith is. It is in him—the only one with the power to protect us and heal us from the struggle of burnout.

5

Hurts So Good

But anyone who drinks the water I give them will never be thirsty. In fact, the water I give them will become a spring of water in them. It will flow up into eternal life.

John 4:14

Y'all, I give you my word, I am not a pyromaniac. But I almost burned down my parents' house the other day. This is a totally true story.

My mom and dad have worked incredibly hard. They are some of the most diligent, giving, and fiscally responsible people I know. As you might expect, they have a beautiful home in Dallas with this incredible outdoor kitchen. It's beyond Insta-worthy. Anyway, my parents were out of town, so I decided to go to their house and use their grill. We had some friends coming over, and I really wanted to cook our grilled chicken over an open flame.

Let me preface what happened next with this—I am a decent cook. It's something I love doing. I cook almost all our meals from scratch. I know that's kind of annoying to all the nonchefs out there, but it's my burden to bear. I cooked the chicken, and it turned out exactly how I wanted—grill marks on both sides. Then I wrapped it up, turned off the burners on the outdoor grill, and went back home to serve my hungry guests. As the kids would say, that chicken was *bussing* (tasty). We had zero leftovers.

The next day I was at a moms' group, and my phone *kept* ringing. I'm not super great at reading texts or responding to calls right away, so I just kept letting it go to voice mail. At some point, I noticed that a few of the missed calls were from a staff member at my parents' church. I was like, *Why would they be trying to get in touch with me?* There were also two missed calls from my twin, Laurie. That was when I got scared. Had something happened to Mom or Dad? I didn't know, so I called her right away.

"What happened?" I demanded as soon as she answered.

"Landra, you left the gas on at Mom and Dad's yesterday."

Immediately, I imagined my parents' house going up in flames. It wasn't a far-fetched dramatization. The gas on their monster-sized grill had been left on all night and the next morning. It wouldn't have taken more than a tiny spark to start a raging fire.

I said, "Are you joking?"

"Nope. Luckily Dad smelled the gas from inside and went out to investigate. If he hadn't . . ."

She didn't have to finish the sentence. You know that feeling when something awful *almost* happens, but then it doesn't? But it's almost like the very thought of it wraps itself around your throat and squeezes? Yeah, that's how I felt. I was completely sick.

Luckily, my parents weren't too upset with me. I mean, I'm probably never allowed to use their grill again, but at least they're still speaking to me.

Have you ever done anything like that? Something so completely thoughtless and stupid that you just feel absolutely *gross* over it? Maybe you bumped into your husband's car while pulling out of the driveway. Or you forgot it was your week to host book club, and everybody showed up to you binge-watching *Real Housewives* in your pajamas. Or you missed your friend's birthday because you're so busy you're not even sure what day of the week it is anymore.

Unintentional mistakes are one thing. We may be embarrassed or ashamed, but everyone forgives us in the end (usually). But intentional mistakes are totally different. When *we* hurt someone on purpose or when someone hurts *us* on purpose, forgiveness is hard to come by. Why? Because it hurts.

It literally *hurts*.

Our bodies interpret emotional pain in much the same way they process physical pain. In 2011, the Pew Research Center did a study where "psychologists used a functional magnetic resonance imaging (fMRI) machine to scan the brains of forty heartbroken participants, all of whom had recently undergone an unwanted breakup."[1] Participants in the study were asked to simultaneously look at photos of the person who rejected them and concentrate on the feelings of rejection they were experiencing during the scanning process. I mean, bold ask, study organizers, but you guys are the experts.

Next, participants were asked to look at photos of close friends while recalling happy moments they shared with those people. Again, while undergoing the same brain scan. Finally, the last test of the study was to scan participants' brains as they experienced pain and pleasure from having objects of various temperatures placed on their arm. The findings were fascinating: "The sight of an ex-partner and the sensation of the hot object activated areas of the brain associated with pain, but the photo of a friend and the pleasant warmth did not. A review of 524 other neuroscience studies on experiences ranging from pain to memory supported the psychologists' results."[2]

The data recorded in a report by the Proceedings of the National Academy of Sciences (PNAS) stated that "the same areas of the brain were associated with pain in up to 88% of the studies they reviewed."[3] So if you're wondering why heartbreak and rejection hurt so much, it's because they do— your brain tells you so.

I'll never forget the first time I felt personally rejected. I really wanted a job at Lululemon. Don't make fun of me—it was a dream of mine. I was in high school at the time, and I went in for a group interview. It was far and away one of the strangest experiences of my life. They had us all sit "criss-cross applesauce" (their words) in a circle while the hiring managers, all decked out like a Lulu brigade, talked to us.

By the end of the interview, I would have taken a bullet for Lululemon. I mean, they were so convincing that it was *the* place to work. So when I got the news that I did *not* get the job, I was devastated. I cried and cried. At the time, I was at a place in my eating disorder where I was binge-eating burgers, so I felt much heavier than "normal." Everyone sitting cross-legged around me had been fit and athletic looking. I convinced myself I wasn't hired because I was a fat slob (I was neither). I felt so completely rejected.

But that wasn't my first round with pain. I experienced rejection on a much larger scale early in my teen years. When a now-infamous (and baseless) news story about my parents broke, it seemed all our "friends" deserted us. That sends a message: you're only worthy of love and acceptance when your public image benefits me. My own pain was immense, but witnessing the wounds of my parents was worse.

Another painful experience was after I was married, when Brad and I moved to Oklahoma to work at a church. I'm sure there are lovely, warm, and welcoming towns in Oklahoma, where anyone would be thrilled to live. Where we moved was not that kind of place. Instead, we were greeted with suspicion from the onset because we were Texans. To heap more coals on our heads, Brad and I had been tasked with taking over a church that was experiencing a bit of crisis. Their former senior pastor had gotten sick, which was so heartbreaking.

A series of circumstances had also led this congregation into a good bit of debt—an insurmountable amount by any standard. Whatever number you're thinking in your head right now? It was more than *that*. The very first thing Brad and I were told to do by trusted financial advisors was to get the payroll down, way down. In fact, there wasn't even enough money to make the next payroll payments.

What a way to start a new job, right? "Hi, we're new here. You're fired."

Brad and I had to have conversations with twenty people to tell them the organization could no longer afford their services to the church. Twenty people had to go home and tell their families. Twenty people had to find new work. Twenty people had one of the worst days of their lives. Brad and I both felt miserable about it. We prayed, we cried. But in the end, there was no choice. I imagine these people felt incredibly hurt and rejected.

Brad and I wanted this church to thrive and grow. We had left my family, the church I'd grown up in, and my home to move there—with a preschooler and a baby on the way. It wasn't like we were just *dying* to leave our previous situation in Texas. We felt the call of God. We prayed (begged) for the wisdom to steer the congregation toward him and toward financial soundness. We'd have loved the opportunity to hire back the staff we had to let go. But from the outside, I can see how we looked like the enemy. At least, at first. I figured that after people got to know us, got to see our hearts, they would accept us.

I remember being at the local playground with Sterling. I was lonelier than I'd ever been. I was deeply craving friendship. I love other moms, and that's all I wanted—a friend. Someone to talk to and relate with. But making friends as a grown-up is hard. It's intimidating! I wish it could be like it was in elementary school, when you had the same color barrettes as someone else, so you were besties for life. Despite my reservations, I scraped together the courage to walk up to another mom and introduce myself.

When I spoke, my voice was shaking. "How old are your kids?"

We exchanged the basic information, and I must have mentioned church because she said, "Oh, where do you go to church?"

I told her and her response was something like, "Oh, *that* church? Did you hear the new pastors there came in and just fired everybody? Can you *believe* that?"

I was alone. The one connection I had made with another girl there fizzled when she up and stopped talking to me randomly. Later, I found out her husband had discouraged her from being my friend because of what was going on at the church. Needless to say, our dream of rebuilding, regrowing, and reviving that congregation went up in flames. Could we have done a better job? Maybe. I'm sure there are things we could have done better. But I'm not sure how.

I was hurt. By God, the church, and the entire state of Oklahoma by the time we left. The ache radiated from the center of my chest as if I'd been physically wounded. Because, according to my brain, I had been.

A few months ago, a bunch of us traveled to Austin, Texas, for a conference. Someone brought up LeeBeth, and my mind randomly started racing. That's how grief works—unexpected, chaotic.

Why did she die?

How did she die, exactly?

Was she in pain?

Questions I won't have the answers to on this side of heaven began to circle in my head like a merry-go-round of madness. It wasn't long before my heart started pounding. I was sweaty and panicky. "Pull over," I told the girl driving. "I think I'm having a heart attack."

I wasn't exaggerating. My chest felt as if it were in a quickly tightening vice grip. I even called 911. It was an all-out tangled mess of emotional and physical pain wreaking havoc on my body.

Pain is painful. That's obvious, right? But isn't it sometimes surprising how much we can hurt on the inside without actually being physically hurt on the outside?

In the book of Ruth in the Bible, we're told about a woman named Naomi. There was a time in her life when Naomi probably felt like she had it all. She was married and had not just one but two sons. But then a famine swept across the land, and Naomi and her family had to leave their hometown of Bethlehem for Moab to escape it. While living in Moab, Naomi's husband died. The Bible tells us that her two sons decided to marry foreign women, which at the time was against the commandment of God to the Israelites (Ezra 10:10). Then, the unthinkable happened—Naomi's sons died too.

Imagine how that must have felt. You're away from home, unable to return or you'll starve to death. Then your husband, the leader of your family, dies. Next, your sons are living wildly, doing whatever they want. Then they die. You're too old to remarry and have more children. You're vulnerable, alone, and without recourse.

I'm trekking right along with Naomi's reaction in Ruth 1 when she says, "Don't call me Naomi. . . . Call me Mara, because the Almighty has made my life very bitter" (v. 20 NIV; *mara* means "bitter"). I don't know about you, but I've been there. You get hurt over and over and over again, so many times that you become this sort of jaded, sarcastic version of who you used to be. And yeah, a lot of the time, it's directed at people. But most of the time, like Naomi, it's ultimately directed at God.

Or consider the story of Joseph in the book of Genesis. Want to talk about someone who'd been rejected by people?

Try being hated by your siblings—all of them. We read that Joseph was his father's favorite. Why? Because Joseph was the baby of the family—until Benjamin showed up, that is. Birth-order favoritism at its finest. See, there really *is* nothing new under the sun.

When Joseph was seventeen, his brothers decided to throw him into the bottom of an empty well and tell their father that a wild animal had eaten him. But just as they had wrestled him inside, they saw some travelers coming from Gilead. His brother Judah had a bright idea: "'What will we gain if we kill our brother and try to cover up what we've done? Come. Let's sell him to these traders. Let's not harm him ourselves. After all, he's our brother. He's our own flesh and blood.' Judah's brothers agreed with him" (Gen. 37:26–27).

In order to spare their own "flesh and blood" from thirsting to death at the bottom of a dry well, they sold him as a slave to complete strangers.

Before you go judging Joseph's brothers, there's a part of the story you don't normally hear preached from the stage. One of the very first things the Bible tells us about Joseph was that he had tattled to Israel about the poor job the brothers were doing caring for the flocks in the field (v. 2). In fact, Israel used Joseph to spy on his brothers and report back on more than one occasion (vv. 13–14).

Then Joseph's father gave him *and only him* a beautiful, colorful robe that Joseph had no issues flaunting in front of his brothers (v. 23). But to top it all off, Joseph had prophetic dreams. Dreams that his brothers and even his entire family would one day bow down to him. Dreams that he shared with all of them. Joseph even annoyed his dad with all his dreaming (v. 10).

Does any of this make what Joseph's brothers did OK? Absolutely not. Let's just make a blanket statement that it's not acceptable to try to murder your sibling, nor is it cool to sell them, regardless of how spoiled, whiny, or superior they act. I don't think Joseph was *malicious* in any of what he did. But he definitely lacked some critical self-awareness.

Joseph's hurt and rejection don't end there. Later in Genesis, we find that Joseph had been purchased by an Egyptian named Potiphar. God was faithful to Joseph and gave him great success as Potiphar's servant. So much so that Potiphar promoted Joseph to his personal assistant, trusting Joseph with everything he owned. We also learn that teenage Joseph had grown up to be a good-looking dude. Which is where Joseph's *next* catastrophe begins.

Apparently, Potiphar's wife had noticed Joseph's attractiveness because we're told she approached her husband's A-1 from day one and said, "Come to bed with me!" (Gen. 39:7). I'm not sure if I'm impressed with her confidence or legitimately creeped out. Probably a little of both.

But Joseph, out of his love for God and respect for Potiphar, flatly refused his boss's wife, saying, "How could I do an evil thing like that?" (v. 9). Ouch. Joseph not only told her no; he also low-key called her evil. When she tried to not-so-gently coax him into bed a second time, Joseph literally *ran* away from her. He hightailed it so quickly that he left his coat in her hands (v. 13). And approximately zero people are surprised to learn that Potiphar's wife decided to get even: "She kept Joseph's coat with her until Potiphar came home. Then she told him her story. She said, 'That Hebrew slave you brought us came to me to rape me. But I screamed for help. So he left his coat beside me and ran out of the house'" (vv. 16–18).

Just like a bad Lifetime movie, Potiphar believed his wife and immediately had Joseph thrown in jail. Without even stopping to ask Joseph—the man he'd trusted with *everything*—his side of the story. Joseph sat in jail, having committed no crime.

Naomi's story didn't end with her being bitter toward God. And Joseph's story didn't end with him enraged at his family or Potiphar. No, both went on to trust God and forgive those who had wronged them.

But the in-between is so *hard*—the days, weeks, months, and years between our pain and our restoration. Pain comes in waves too. You may not have healed from your last hurt when another one smacks you upside the heart. In the moment, how we feel seems so much bigger than anything else that could potentially *be*. We can't imagine a time in the near or distant future when we'll stop feeling wounded.

We've all experienced pain, hurt, and rejection. In fact, I bet if you open your favorite music app and look up the top songs of today, most of them are about some sort of emotional pain or trauma. Being a Christian doesn't make us immune. It doesn't even make us less likely to get hurt. Pain is as much a part of life as waking and breathing.

Maybe, like Ruth, you've lost someone you love. A spouse or a child or, like me, a sister. Or you've felt like an outsider or suffered feelings of abandonment. Or maybe, like Joseph, someone has wronged you. They've wronged you *bad*. You find it hard to trust people—maybe even hard to trust God. Or like Brad and I in Oklahoma, maybe you gave something your best effort, prayed, and committed your plans to God . . . and it still didn't work out. You ended up hurt and rejected.

Gosh, it *hurts*. Not just mentally but also physically. But what's the point? Why? Why does God allow us to go through so much pain? Why can't he find a more acceptable, less uncomfortable way to grow and teach us? Well, for one, human nature puts us at risk of repeating the same pattern over and over until something disrupts and changes that pattern. And frankly, humans are too stubborn or selfish to make a change until deciding otherwise costs them something.

I think we can all see *some* good in suffering pain and rejection. You've probably heard quotes, stories, and Scriptures about how pain can benefit us. But there's still the issue of the aching, the hurting, the feelings of bitterness and cynicism. What are we to do with all of that?

I think if we were all honest, we'd be able to see that we share some of the blame for our pain. Now, before you fling this book (or whatever device you may be reading it on) to the ground, hear me out.

It's been my personal experience that part of my problem is my tendency to depend on people for what I should be getting from God. I depend on others to affirm me, forgive me, love me, be honest with me, and define me. Basically, I wake up every morning with an empty cup. I take that cup to Brad to pour into. I take it to my kids. I take my cup to work. I for sure take it with me on Instagram. When I'm with my family or friends? You bet that cup is held out, waiting to get filled. And when someone doesn't have enough water to top off my cup—or even worse, when they pour in *dirty* water? *Game over*. I throw that cup and stomp my feet like a toddler out of her favorite juice.

I saw this play out in my precious sister's life too. I'm definitely not a doctor, and I never confirmed my theory with

LeeBeth personally, but I believe most of her sickness sprang from the pain of rejection. Growing up, LeeBeth was a rule follower. She was conservative when it came to dating. Me, on the other hand? Your girl was straight-up boy crazy. But not LeeBeth. She had one serious boyfriend when she was younger, and she practiced purity in that relationship with total confidence. But when that relationship ended and Lee-Beth got older, she dated with one goal in mind—marriage.

And that marriage for LeeBeth never came.

Let me ask you a question: Who (or what) are you bringing your "cup" of life to? The Bible already tells us that Jesus is the only source that will satisfy: "But anyone who drinks the water I give them will never be thirsty. In fact, the water I give them will become a spring of water in them. It will flow up into eternal life" (John 4:14).

When we're hurting, in pain, and wounded, it sucks. It just does. That's normal. That's *human*. Take a beat. Don't ignore what you're feeling. Don't tell yourself, *Oh, I shouldn't feel this way—I'm a Christian.* But at the same time, don't sit in it either. Get to work on your wounds.

That starts by reframing your hurts. Stop and ask yourself why you're hurting the way you are. Have you placed too much emphasis on a relationship, job, or status? Have you defined yourself based on anything other than the Bible's words about who you are? Are you expecting people to be perfect at all times?

I've been there. I expect those around me to be perfect. I also expect my life circumstances to be perfect. I bet you do the same thing. You may not be aware of it. I mean, I imagine that none of us go around thinking, *Life is perfect, people are good, and nothing bad is going to happen today.*

91

No, but when we *do* get hurt, when we *do* get rejected, and when people or God *do* disappoint us, we're shocked.

In other words, when humans act human, we act human in return. Sometimes, simply acknowledging that messiness and suffering are unavoidable by-products of the human condition makes our pain just a little less isolating. No, we can't live a pain-free life, but we can control pain's meaning in our life. We can control the amount of influence our wounds have on us, giving ourselves a sense of purpose and power. Conversely, we could live out of woundedness, devaluing our purpose and feeling chronically powerless. Instead of letting pain lead, let's take charge instead.

Let's practice. Say your spouse cheats on you. No, you can*not* end up on the next episode of *Dateline*. I mean, I love the show, but let someone else give them content. So you find out you've been betrayed. Take a minute to wallow. Scream, cry, eat all the things. But at some point, the fog has to lift. *You* have to lift. You have to lift yourself. Ask yourself a couple of questions:

> What does his cheating change about who God says
> I am? *Nothing.*
> What does his cheating change about who God is?
> *Nothing.*

> Did you lose your job?

> What does this loss change about who God says I am?
> *Nothing.*
> What does this loss change about who God is? *Nothing.*

I know that when you line up any hurt, pain, or rejection against these two truths, the power, love, and consistency of God will always win. Because of that, you can find healing. Because of him, you can have hope. With these two truths leading your life, you will begin to recover in a meaningful way, far sooner than you would if you allowed your suffering to determine the rest of your life.

God provides a respite for our pain through the comfort of his Holy Spirit. He also gives us a safeguard against pain—his undying love and acceptance of us. When we can bring our cup of life directly to him—today and every day—the troubles of this world sting a bit less because we're firmly rooted in the knowledge of just who our deliverer is. Our deliverer is not humanity. Our deliverer is not money. Our deliverer is not status.

Our deliverer from all pain is our almighty God, who has already defeated death, hell, and the grave, and who has promised to rescue us when we call on him.

6

We All Fall Down

Here is a saying that you can trust. It should be accepted
completely. Christ Jesus came into the world to save sinners.
And I am the worst sinner of all. But for that very reason,
God showed me mercy. And I am the worst of sinners. He
showed me mercy so that Christ Jesus could show that he is
very patient. I was an example for those who would come to
believe in him. Then they would receive eternal life.

1 Timothy 1:15–16

LeeBeth and I almost got my twin sister, Laurie, kid-
napped in London. OK, not really. But maybe. We were all in
a hotel together, and Laurie was going through this phase of
being extremely disciplined with her sleep. I don't remember
why; maybe she'd just read a blog or article online about the
importance of consistent sleep. We were in college at the
time, and in college, whatever new health trend emerges,
you automatically have to try it. I think her militant sleep
regimen was something like that.

Anyway, LeeBeth and I were sharing a room with Laurie, and we had a major case of giggles. Anything was funny. Fly on the wall? Hilarious. Shadow on the floor? Incredibly comedic. Laurie was like our dorm mother. She kept hissing at us and telling us to be quiet. She was beyond irritated. And the more she shushed us, the louder we were and the angrier she got. That's why God gave us siblings, right? To remind us of our humanity.

Laurie lectured us over and over about going to bed. "I can hear you!" she whisper-yelled at us from across the room. Which, of course, just made our quiet laughter transform into obnoxious snorts.

Finally, Princess Laurie was able to fall asleep. But the fun was far from over, because LeeBeth had an idea.

"Let's prank Laurie." LeeBeth had the wildest imagination. That's what made her so creative. Her mind was playful and dynamic. A mystery so beautiful to all who knew her well. So LeeBeth got on the phone and called the front desk. She told them we had a super-early flight—4:00 a.m.—and that it was *imperative* someone give our room a wake-up call. The room Laurie was running a sleep clinic in.

The next morning at breakfast, LeeBeth and I were waiting for Laurie like two kids at Christmas. She sat down, clearly exhausted, and said, "Some man was banging on the door in the middle of the night."

LeeBeth and I dissolved into a fit of laughter. My mom, on the other hand, did not.

"What?" she asked. "Explain to me what happened." She had her I'm-the-mama-bear-and-I-will-roar face on.

Apparently, Laurie hadn't answered the 4:00 a.m. wake-up call, and that front desk must have had the most enthusiastic employees ever because they sent a guy to our room who knocked on the door until Laurie answered. LeeBeth and I had slept through the entire thing.

My parents were absolutely livid at LeeBeth and me. "Do you understand how dangerous that was?" they asked us. "Three young girls in a foreign country with a man at your door?"

At the time, it was still pretty funny to LeeBeth and me. But it wasn't long before a sick sort of feeling settled in. What could have happened was far worse than what did happen. What if the hotel employee had had less-than-proper intentions? What if he'd gotten into our room? What if he'd brought someone up with him? What if . . . ? There were so many possibilities, but trust me, each and every one ran through my head.

I'd messed up. This "mess-up" didn't have many consequences—outside of my mom and dad giving Lee and I *the look* for the remainder of our time in London. But I'd definitely messed up. I'd taken a joke about ten steps too far. That prank could have been next week's *True Crime* podcast's headline. I'm not even sure if I ever apologized. Laurie, when you read this, I'm sorry! Super glad you weren't Bryan Mills's next client.

We all mess up, right? Or maybe a better way to word that is to say we all fail. Because, really, "we messed up" is just a nice way to say that we failed. But we don't say that, do we? We don't like to label our missteps as failures because failure is such a big word. Maybe it gets a bad rap for being the very worst grade we can make in school. Maybe it was also those #EpicFail memes we had to endure. But *fail* sounds way harsher than *mess up*.

I've definitely *failed* before. I failed freshman biology actually. My parents sent us to a private Christian school, and when I came home with an F on my report card, my mom said, "Landra. You do understand that we paid hard-earned money for that F, right?"

I hadn't thought of that at the time. In fact, I was far more interested in friends and guys than I was in biology (hence, the failure). When she worded it *that* way, I felt like a double failure. The icing on my cake of failure was summer school. I had never considered the fact that not doing my work during the school year meant I would have to do it during the summer. But that's what happened—three weeks of summer school while my friends were hanging out.

I don't know about you, but I experience feelings of failure pretty often. When I get on social media and see other people's weekends with their families? They've taken their kids to a professional sporting event, cooked their spouse a seven-course brunch, created adorable Mama and Mini tees (organic cotton, duh), and gone on at least one family hike in matching flannels. I look at our wild weekends as church staff and think, *My poor children. They'll never enjoy a carefree Saturday and Sunday.* Because Sunday is always coming. I feel like a failure as a parent.

I felt like a failure after my first book, *A Different Kind of Love Story*, came out. The book did well—don't get me wrong. I guess I just had high expectations. My dad is a *New York Times* bestselling author, so those expectations were probably (definitely) unrealistic.

But I felt like I was really putting myself out there. Telling the world you went to rehab for an eating disorder is a little like standing naked in the streets of New York City. I had all these dates lined up to go speak at churches and other events—and I was so excited to meet everyone. To hear their stories. To connect.

But then, COVID.

I really don't need to say more, do I? I'm sure we all have a story in which its miserable pivot point is "But then, COVID." What a mess COVID made.

It goes without saying, there was no book tour. There were no meet and greets. Pretty much every date and engagement was canceled, and we were left scrambling to figure out how to handle it. There are no blogs on promoting your first book during a pandemic. In a lot of ways, surface ways, if I'm honest, that book felt like a failure.

There are different kinds of mess ups, right? Different kinds of failures. Maybe even different levels of failure based on its consequences. And those consequences are measured by how much suffering they cause. If we fail and no one notices, it doesn't bother us nearly as much as if we fail and *everyone* notices.

There are failures that aren't really failures. These are perceived failures. Parents, we know all about these. Like the social media example I shared, any time it seems that someone is doing more or doing better than us as parents, the sense of failure settles into our chests and takes up residence. If we don't get the opportunity at work we wanted, it feels like failure. If we aren't invited to an outing our friends are at, it feels like failure. If COVID ruins our first book release—a book that we poured out the dark places of our hearts to write—that most definitely feels like a failure.

Then there are the more obvious failures. Those by anyone's standards—moral failures like affairs, stealing, lying.

They are the big price tag failures—the ones that cost us a lot. We place these types of failures in their own category. These are the failures that get whispered about in church bathrooms and texted about behind closed doors.

Any American literature fans here? I remember in high school having to read *The Scarlet Letter* by Nathaniel Hawthorne. Maybe you've seen the movie version with Demi Moore. Even if you have no idea what the story line is about, you may have heard the title used in reference to someone who has failed and is being publicly shamed.

The book is set in a Puritan colony back in the 1600s. The main character, Hester Prynne, has an affair with the town's priest and becomes pregnant. Her indiscretion is especially noticeable as her husband has not yet joined her in the colony and is presumed dead. When she's found out, Hester is forced to wear a scarlet-colored *A* embroidered to the front of her dress to indicate to everyone that she is an adulteress.

Can you imagine if society still operated this way? There's not enough thread in the world.

Hester's moral failure was put on display for all to see. The *A* was meant to be a symbol of shame for Hester to wear as punishment. But by the end of the book, the *A* had taken on a completely different meaning. Hester had overcome her failures—in fact, she'd leveraged her mess-up until the *A* no longer reminded people that she'd been an adulteress but that she was able: able to be a single mother to her child, able to endure public humiliation, and able to find happiness in a world that treated her with indifference and ridicule.

We read the story of the Puritans who were so judgmental that they banished Hester to a lifetime of public shame because she became pregnant outside of marriage. We think,

How extreme. How rigid. How cruel! But the thing is we kind of do the same thing. We do this to others, and we do this to ourselves.

We label ourselves as failures. We put a big scarlet letter on ourselves. Instead of allowing our failures to inform our future, we allow our failures to limit the future.

I believe my and LeeBeth's addictions were fueled by feelings of failure. For LeeBeth, because she wasn't married, because she hadn't accomplished more professionally, but especially because she viewed her alcohol abuse as a failure. And that's the strange thing about addiction, because we're told it's a sickness and a disease, and studies support this as fact. "In 2011, the American Society of Addiction Medicine (ASAM) joined the AMA (American Medical Association) defining addiction as a chronic brain disorder, not a behavioral problem, or just the result of making bad choices."[1] Addiction "rewires" the human brain to repeat patterns and behaviors that result in pleasure.[2] Our brains have reward systems that are fueled by a neurotransmitter called dopamine. Essentially, dopamine communicates to the brain, "Whatever you just did, it felt good. You should do it again." When you're an addict, your "drug of choice" releases spurts of dopamine, only in much larger amounts than it would after normal, healthy behaviors. "For the brain, the difference between normal rewards and drug rewards can be likened to the difference between someone whispering into your ear and someone shouting into a microphone."[3]

When you take a drink, pop a pill, binge and purge, or swipe that credit card, your dopamine levels spike. You feel immediate euphoria. But these false sources of dopamine fuel your body, and you start producing less of your own natural dopamine. Because it's being flooded with the chemical each time you're triggered.

Our society views addicts as failures when really they're (we're) sick people with a highly dysfunctional disease. But we reduce people who suffer—and trust me, we suffer—from any sort of addiction to weak, irresponsible, worthless addicts. One reason I'm sharing so openly about my sister is because I refuse to let her death be in vain. I pray her story puts a face to a disease so many hide for fear of being judged as failures.

If you or someone you know is suffering from any sort of addiction, come out of the shadows. You're not a failure. You're sick. If you had strep throat, you'd take an antibiotic, wouldn't you? If you had cancer, you'd get radiation and chemotherapy. If you're sick with any type of addiction, there are free, discreet ways to get help. I'd start with an internet search. There are remote recovery meetings held online at any given moment of the day.

Failure, whether it's actual failure or perceived failure, does not have to be fatal. It does not mean we have to wear a scarlet letter forever. And it does not mean that we are condemned to a life of suffering. Yes, sometimes the consequences of our failures hurt, but how long they hurt and to what degree that hurt influences the rest of our lives is really up to us.

There are some great examples of failures in the Bible.[4] If you've been in church very long, you've probably already heard all the stories I'm about to reference. But if you're anything like me, you've heard these stories so often that you kind of feel detached from them. It's almost as if they're about make-believe characters from a fairy tale. But as I share these stories with you, I want you to pretend you've never heard them before. Pretend I'm telling you about a mutual friend you lost touch with.

The first story, and probably the most obvious, is the story of David. In something out of an episode of *Bachelor in Paradise*, David was a handsome, successful king who fell for a married woman. And when I say he fell for her, I mean he saw her naked a couple of times and had to have her. Let me remind you—this is the same David who bravely fought Goliath, patiently endured the wickedness of Saul, and had a ride-or-die bond with his bestie, Jonathan. Having trouble reconciling the beloved David with the same man who broke more than half of God's commandments? Welcome to humanity.

In 2 Samuel 11, we learn that David wanted Bathsheba, which was inconvenient because Bathsheba was married to Uriah (vv. 2–3). But David wanted what he wanted, so he took Bathsheba for his own and slept with her (v. 4), claiming her for himself. Then, as is typical with sin, David had to do a little more sinning to aid him in further sinning. But this sin cycle eventually led David to have Uriah murdered (2 Sam. 12:9).

Well, dang. That escalated quickly. It's notable that David didn't make excuses for his sins, as we're often tempted to do. "Well, she was parading around on the roof taking baths! She's a tease! What was I supposed to do? I'm a dude, all right? That's just how we are!" No, David immediately repented and asked for forgiveness. David went on to write numerous psalms about the goodness, love, and mercy of God. But most telling, God chose to make Jesus a direct descendant of David. I'd say David recovered just fine.

The lesson we learn from David's story is that admitting our failures is the fastest way to begin recovery. And not just admitting them but also doing something different. In other words, not repeating the failure over and over again. Not blaming our failures on someone or something else. But owning them *and* their consequences. That's key. When we experience the consequences of our failures, we sometimes feel as if God is punishing us, making us suffer. But that's not how God works.

There are, however, natural consequences to our actions. You've heard the saying "You reap what you sow." If you are unfaithful to your partner and they leave you? That's a natural consequence. If you overspend and can't get approved for a mortgage? That's a natural consequence. If you spend half your workday on Instagram and don't get new opportunities at work? That's a natural consequence.

If you're experiencing the consequences of a failure right now, I'm sorry. I've been there and it sucks. It's OK to say that it's uncomfortable. Maybe embarrassing. Definitely frustrating. But like David, ask God to meet you in your mess. Ask him what you can learn from where you are. Ask him to move you to recovery.

It's easy for us to remember Paul as the great church planter and author of much of the New Testament. But before Paul was Paul, he was Saul of Tarsus. And Saul of Tarsus was, in short, a murderer.

Did Paul regret the things he'd done when he was Saul? Did he feel like a failure for not recognizing the deity of Jesus sooner? You tell me. Here's what he wrote in a letter to Timothy:

Here is a saying that you can trust. It should be accepted completely. Christ Jesus came into the world to save sinners.

And I am the worst sinner of all. But for that very reason, God showed me mercy. And I am the worst of sinners. He showed me mercy so that Christ Jesus could show that he is very patient. I was an example for those who would come to believe in him. Then they would receive eternal life. (1 Tim. 1:15–16)

"I am the worst sinner of all." Have you ever felt that way before? Have you ever looked back on your past choices, decisions, and actions and burned with shame over who you used to be? You're in good company. But we learn from Paul that God can use anyone to further his kingdom, despite past failures. In fact, God purposely picked out Paul on that road to Damascus to display the completeness of the compassionate mercy he has for all of us.

Don't allow the failures of your past to cause you suffering today. Bring your regret, pain, and shame to the foot of the cross and leave it there. Jesus's sacrifice has already paid the price for it. Don't make yourself pay for it too.

In the book of Judges, we are introduced to one of the most interesting people in all of the Bible—Samson. One day his future mother was visited by an angel who basically said, "I know you haven't been able to have kids yet, but here's the thing—you're about to have one. It's a boy. Don't drink wine. Don't eat unclean food. When the kid is born, don't cut his hair. He's going to help save Israel from the Philistines" (see Judg. 13:3–5).

The drama didn't end there. Samson grew up to be a strong, fierce Israelite leader, known for ripping city gates *and* their posts out of the ground and hoisting them on his shoulders like bags of flour (16:3). Fearing Samson's might and influence, the Philistines wanted him dead.

They targeted his weak spot—women. Even though he was already married, Samson couldn't seem to get enough time with female company. We're told that Samson fell in love with a woman named Delilah. Seeing this, the Philistines pulled Delilah aside and offered her silver in exchange for the secret to Samson's superhuman strength.

Remember what the angel said about his hair? That it was never to be cut? If it were, he would lose his power. This was the secret Delilah was after. And after some very *Bachelor*-worthy pouting, Delilah got what she wanted and handed Samson over to the Philistines by shaving the braids off his head.

Hairless Samson was dragged out into a great crowd of his captors to serve as jester. Thousands of people crowded around, cheering and jeering at the fallen strongman. In a scene straight out of a movie, Samson asked God to give him strength one last time.

> Then Samson reached toward the two pillars that were in the middle of the temple. They were the ones that held up the temple. He put his right hand on one of them. He put his left hand on the other. He leaned hard against them. Samson said, "Let me die together with the Philistines!" Then he pushed with all his might. The temple came down on the rulers. It fell on all the people in it. So Samson killed many more Philistines when he died than he did while he lived. (Judg. 16:29–30)

Samson's failure cost him his life. But there's a valuable lesson to be learned: God can overcome our sin to accomplish his purpose for his people. Though I doubt we'll find ourselves dragged into a colosseum gladiator-style, we will likely find ourselves sitting in the consequences of our sin at some point. Like Samson, I encourage you to call out to God. To ask him to use you anyway to accomplish his will.

The last story of failure I want to talk about is one I can especially relate to. It's the prophet Elijah's story.

After Elijah humiliated King Ahab by asking God to use his power to burn Ahab's altar, Ahab and his queen, Jezebel, were furious. They may have also taken offense to the fact that Elijah had all their prophets slaughtered following this altercation, but that's just an assumption.

When Jezebel found out what Elijah had done, she issued a threat to Elijah: "You can be sure that I will kill you, just as I killed the other prophets. I'll do it by this time tomorrow" (1 Kings 19:2).

Jezebel was something else, right? Just penciling in to the itinerary a little homicide as if it were no big deal. Well, to her, it wasn't. Elijah knew Jezebel's anger was dangerous. So what do you think Elijah did? Do you think Elijah showed courage and honor, standing up to Jezebel and daring her to touch one of God's chosen? No, that is not at all what Elijah did.

Elijah took off. He fled to a faraway place and hid under a bush to take a nap. I don't know why this is so funny to me, but it is. How many times as a mother have I felt so burned out, so exhausted, so terrified of facing another day of the constant pressure that I've considered running away just to take a nap? It's more often than you might think.

Not only was Elijah afraid, but he was also exhausted. He said, "Lord, I've had enough" and even prayed for God to take his life (v. 4).

As a prophet, Elijah was a high-profile God follower. People watched what he did and said. To him, it probably felt as if he were going from event to event, having to be "on" and "perform" with no end in sight. So he had an emotional breakdown of sorts—he just gave up.

We've all been in Elijah's sandals. It feels like everywhere we go someone expects something out of us. For Elijah, that was to perform miracles of God. For us, that might look a *little* different. Our jobs, our kids, our churches, our friend groups, social media . . . it's like the entire world is standing in front of us with their hands stuck out, waiting to see just how much they can get from us.

We get tired. The pressure is overwhelming. And we want to give up. Run away. Start over. Hide. Isolate. We feel like we'll never measure up. We feel like failures.

But instead of suffering, let's do what Elijah did. First, he rested. We've already talked about the importance of resting. Resting isn't an admission of weakness. In fact, it takes a self-aware, confident person to know when they need a time-out. After resting, Elijah obeyed God. He did the next right thing, trusting God to give him what he needed, knowing that he wasn't alone.

I was online recently and saw that people are now making "Failure Résumés" and posting them online: "Didn't get the partnership"; "2012–2018: Zero Promotions"; "Applied to 12 medical schools, was rejected by 11."

If you have time later, you should google it. In a world of highlight reels, it's refreshing. The idea that everyone fails at some point in their lives is fairly easy for us to accept. On the other hand, knowing that we will fail isn't so simply embraced. That dichotomy doesn't really make sense, does it? Well, it's due to a shift in perspective. No one plans to fail, so when it happens, it catches us off guard.

Consider the following individuals:

Abraham Lincoln
J. K. Rowling
Ludwig van Beethoven
Michael Jordan
Lady Gaga
Vera Wang
Steven Spielberg
Walt Disney
Oprah Winfrey
Vincent van Gogh

Regardless of what you think about these people as individuals, you have to respect their achievements and legacies. But did you know that each person on this list, at some point or another, experienced failure? Massive failure! And yet they're remembered by the majority as great or successful in their own right. Want to know why? They didn't let their failure become the end of their story. They kept pushing, trying, and believing.

All saccharine sayings aside, failure is inevitable. It's not some slogan on a T-shirt. It's real life, and it hurts. But failure is also one of our greatest teachers and motivators. I could list many more highly successful people who failed at many things, many times. Yes, when we fail, we sometimes suffer as a result. But there are ways to work ourselves through those feelings while still appreciating the lessons learned.

Read the resiliency promised us in Jeremiah 8:4:

> Jeremiah, tell them, "The LORD says,
> 'When people fall down, don't they get up again?
>   When someone turns away, don't they come
>   back?'"

God's good purpose is *not* that you fail. It's bigger than that.

In her blog post "God Permits What He Hates," Joni Eareckson Tada says, "Sometimes God permits what He hates to accomplish that which He loves."[5] Maybe you are suffering and need to read that right now. God hates suffering. If you study the ministry of Christ, you see that almost everything he did miracle-wise was to relieve some sort of suffering.

No, God does not want you to fail. He wants what's on the other side of that failure. He wants you to turn to him. To repent, if that's what's needed. He wants you to be honest. He wants to restore you to a position of capable influence. God wants to be the God of your victories. But he especially wants to be the God of your failures.

7

Slaying the Giant

Do not let your hearts be troubled. You believe in God. Believe in me also. There are many rooms in my Father's house. If this were not true, would I have told you that I am going there? Would I have told you that I would prepare a place for you there? If I go and do that, I will come back. And I will take you to be with me. Then you will also be where I am. You know the way to the place where I am going.

John 14:1–4

LeeBeth could be intimidating. She had a fierce personality. If she was on your side, you felt undefeatable. If she was *not* on your side . . . you were a little worried. I guess you could say we had the typical big sister/little sister dynamic. I would terrorize her, and she would lash out at me. Especially when it had to do with me going into her bedroom.

Why is your older sibling's bedroom the coolest place on earth when you're a kid? If you didn't have an older sibling, it's going to be hard to understand. But there's something mysterious and wonderful about their bedroom. As if that's the place you can go to figure out how to act older and wiser. Anyway, LeeBeth had a beautiful canopy bed in her room. I was obsessed with it. Once, I snuck in there just to jump on it. Doesn't that sound smart? No, Landra. Not smart at all.

I must have really been testing the mattress's limits because somehow my foot hit the middle of a bar on the canopy and it snapped, collapsing the entire canopy on top of the bed like a pink lace graveyard. I love how irrational little kids' minds can be. I remember thinking, *If I just prop the bars on the end of the bed, maybe she won't notice.* But it didn't work. It was no use. It was a destruction zone. And I was scared, really and truly afraid of what LeeBeth would do or say when she found out.

Turns out, I was spot-on. LeeBeth hit the roof. She was livid. But LeeBeth was also smart. She didn't yell and scream and pitch a fit for all to hear. No, she retaliated behind closed doors. She bided her time, waiting a few days before she came into *my* room and glued all my stuffed animals together. She didn't stop there. No, she took it to a whole other level. She broke Samantha's leg. You know Samantha—the American Girl Doll whose price tag was only topped by her desirableness. This was long before the days when you could buy generic accessories and dolls. And LeeBeth knew I loved my Samantha.

I was devastated. My mom made LeeBeth pay to send Samantha to the American Girl Doll hospital to get a little refresher. (Yes, the store offers hospital visits for its dolls and their accessories when terrifying older sisters strike.) When Samantha returned, she was wearing a cast and had crutches.

So yeah, LeeBeth was a formidable force. I was definitely wary of crossing her again after that. But I didn't live in *fear* of LeeBeth, though I've had plenty of fears in my life—some more random than others. Take sharks, for example. I know, I know, it's such a basic fear. Who *isn't* fearful of sharks? That would be a much shorter list! But I actually have a good reason.

Ed Young is a huge fisherman. If you know my dad, you know he loves to be on the water. When I was nine or ten years old, he took me out fishing. We weren't on a very big boat—an offshore boat of maybe twenty feet. Anyway, it was me, my dad, and a fishing guide. My dad was standing at the bow of the boat with his line out. Then, like it sometimes does, his line snapped down into the water.

"I've got one!" he called to us. I could hear in his voice that he was already straining against the pull of the line.

The guide and I went to the front of the boat where my dad was. Whatever he'd caught, it was big, wild, and angry. My dad struggled with his rod.

"You need to move to the middle of the boat," the guide told him, "before you tip over the bow."

My dad shuffled toward the center, wrestling his catch with every move.

Then movement to my right caught my eye. I stopped watching my dad and looked. There it was—a fin. A dorsal fin. Dorsal fin sharks are easy to identify. Their fins are almost like a serrated knife because of a little horn-like "spine" they have at their base. Yuck. I'm cringing just thinking about it.

My dad's catch was losing blood. And that blood had apparently been a dinner invitation to our new shark guest.

I watched with a growing sense of panic as the shark circled our boat. Around and around and around. You might be thinking, *What's the big deal? You're on a boat and the shark is in the water!* But you don't understand. It felt like the shark was as big as the boat. (It wasn't.) Then the shark pushed itself out of the water, all 73,000 of his razor teeth bared. He was huge! Like, twelve feet long at least.

I remember thinking, *I will never put a toe in the ocean again. That's it—the ocean is ruined for me now. I am no longer naive to what lives down there.* Seeing a shark eye-to-eye was a loss-of-innocence moment for me. Sharks are worthy of my fear.

I've experienced other types of fear too, more phobia related than actual terror. Hair is one—loose hair anywhere. I can't handle it. If I check in to a hotel and there is one strand of hair in my room, I want to vomit. My hair phobia could be related to a deeper anxiety. When I was at my sickest, making myself throw up multiple times a day, my hair started to fall out. I'd get in the shower and feel the deepest dread because I knew when I got out, there'd be a clump of lost hair in the drain.

Dread. That's another type of fear. I imagine we've all lived with a lingering sense of dread since early 2020 when news of the first COVID-19 case marked an entirely new way of life for the entire world. There was a minute there when I was fearful I might never get toilet paper again. Grocery stores looked like a scene from a postapocalyptic zombie movie. We were all told to wear masks, stay home, and wait it out. I don't know about you, but I'm not a very good wait-er. I have this slightly anxious energy that simmers in lethargy. But a quarantine? I was a bubbling cauldron of fear.

Since then, most days feel like the world has devolved into a series of chaotic events. Nothing has been the same. Not since 9/11 have I ever felt the fear I experience now. The fear that our country may not ever recover. The fear to voice my own convictions.

What a time to be alive, y'all. It's wild.

Fears are powerful. I don't think I have to convince you of that. Fear can transform us into angry people, quiet people, dysfunctional people, judgmental people, or apathetic people. Something you never hear? "Fear turned me into a happy, peaceful, productive person. I'm so thankful for my fear!" Fears paralyze us. They grip us. And yes, they cause us to suffer.

Human beings have always held certain fears. And for the most part, we've basically always feared the same stuff.

In my experience, one of the biggest fears of humankind is the fear of failure. I just wrote an entire chapter on why, but I think the heart of this fear is less specific than we may realize. I think we fear never realizing our full potential. We fear being unhappy because we haven't reached our goals. We fear the general way that failure feels.

Moses feared failure. In Exodus, we read of the many excuses he gave to God when God asked Moses to be his mouthpiece to the enslaved Israelites:

The LORD said, "I have seen how my people are suffering in Egypt. I have heard them cry out because of their slave drivers. I am concerned about their suffering. So I have come down to save them from the Egyptians. I will bring them up out of that land. I will bring them into a good land. It has a lot of room. It is a land that has plenty of milk and honey.

The Canaanites, Hittites, Amorites, Perizzites, Hivites and Jebusites live there. And now Israel's cry for help has reached me. I have seen how badly the Egyptians are treating them. So now, go. I am sending you to Pharaoh. I want you to bring the Israelites out of Egypt. They are my people."

But Moses spoke to God. "Who am I that I should go to Pharaoh?" he said. "Who am I that I should bring the Israelites out of Egypt?" (3:7–11)

Moses said to God, "Suppose I go to the people of Israel. Suppose I say to them, 'The God of your fathers has sent me to you.' And suppose they ask me, 'What is his name?' Then what should I tell them?" (v. 13)

Moses answered, "What if the elders of Israel won't believe me? What if they won't listen to me? Suppose they say, 'The Lord didn't appear to you.' Then what should I do?" (4:1)

Moses spoke to the Lord. He said, "Lord, I've never been a good speaker. And I haven't gotten any better since you spoke to me. I don't speak very well at all" (v. 10)

Oh, Moses. You sound like Sterling when I ask her to pick up her toys. Excuse after excuse after excuse. Moses had a stutter. He felt inadequate to bring God's people into the promised land. But God appeared to Moses in a fantastic way—a bush on fire. I'm pretty sure God knows what he's doing. He hadn't accidentally happened upon Moses. He chose him. And still, Moses feared failure. It's a fear many of us experience today.

I wonder what excuses we've made out of fear of failure. "But I don't have the time to start a podcast." "I can't write a book. I suck at Instagram captions." "What if I'm vulnerable and open up to people but they can't relate?" Those are some of my most recent excuses. If God is calling you to do something, don't be like me and Moses. Have faith that if he's called you, he's going with you. Don't give your fear more power than you give God.

Another one of our common, shared fears is the fear of loss. The fear of loss is tricky. I immediately think of my kids. Or Brad. If I were to lose one of them, y'all would have to come scrape me up off the floor. But I think the fear of loss plays out in many subtle ways too. I want you to think about the last time you were really angry. The last time you were just downright ticked off. Then I want you to ask yourself, "What was I afraid of losing?" I bet if you dig deep, you'll see that the fear of loss is most evident in our lives when we're mad.

Let me give you an example. And this is super petty, so feel free to judge me. I was in line at the drive-through at Chick-fil-A. The line was absurd, but I'm pregnant and no longer in control of my body. If it tells me it wants a chicken sandwich, it gets a chicken sandwich.

There's a line in the road before the line in the parking lot. And, like God-fearing grown-ups, we're all taking turns, letting cars in from both directions. Left lane turns in, then right lane turns in. We learned this skill in preschool. When it came to my turn to pull into the parking lot, a cute little BMW in the other lane shot in front of me. *That's two cars in a row from the same lane.*

I'm not a horn honker, but I might have given that Beamer a little toot if the kids hadn't been with me. When I think about it, what made me so angry wasn't just that the driver didn't follow the rules, but they made me feel that they won something I lost. We're talking about a spot in a drive-through, but I think the principle applies to a lot of scenarios.

Losing money? Losing time? Losing respect? Losing opportunities? These are all things that can make us spit fire, we're so mad. To avoid the rage that the feeling of losing gives us, we protect ourselves. We hedge our bets. We don't open up completely. We don't put ourselves out there more. We don't take chances because we don't want to lose.

When it comes to losing loved ones or being hurt by a loved one, the fear of loss causes us to suffer from anxiety. We lose sleep over our children. We grow suspicious of our friends and partners. We become someone others have a difficult time being around because we're terrorized by our fear of the pain of loss.

When we fear loss, we're like David in the Bible. David's fear of loss was so great, he feared that darkness would overtake him (Ps. 139:11). Yes, darkness may come; it does for all of us at some point. But God is our light in the darkness: "Even the darkness is not dark to you; the night is bright as the day, for darkness is as light with you" (v. 12 ESV).

What do you fear losing? Your parents? Your husband? Your baby? These are real, serious fears. I am not making light of them. Losing LeeBeth was a vague fear I had in those last years. Maybe that's why I was so irritated with her by the time she died. Maybe I was subconsciously distancing myself from her. I'm not sure I ever thought she would really *die*. And in many ways, I had already lost my sister as I knew her. But, yes, LeeBeth died, and it hurt like hell.

Here's what I'm learning about actual loss that might help us with our fear of potential loss. We don't understand death. We just don't get it. That makes sense, though, because none of us have died. Sure, some have been clinically dead for a few minutes. I've heard those harrowing experiences, and they always fascinate me. But a true life-to-death experience in the long term has not been documented since biblical times. So if we want to know the truth about the afterlife, we have to look to the author of life in the pages of his Word.

Our eternal home, heaven, is a real place (John 14:1–3) where we will live in real, physical bodies (1 Cor. 15). There, we will experience everlasting joy, rewards, and treasures (Matt. 5:12; 6:19–20; Luke 6:23). Heaven is where God lives (Rev. 21:3), and the light of Jesus will illuminate the entire place (Rev. 22:5).

In heaven, we will see the Lord "face to face" (1 Cor. 13:12). There will be no evil (Rev. 21:27), no more sickness, crying, or pain (Rev. 21:4). In fact, we're told that those who love God can't even imagine how wonderful and peaceful life in eternity will be (1 Cor. 2:9).

In heaven, we'll finally have an end to racism and prejudice. There won't be a hint of pride, jealousy, discrimination, or competition. People from "every nation, tribe and people" will be there, worshiping God side by side in harmony (Rev. 7:9). We won't, in fact, be diaper-wearing cherubs singing hymns all day but will learn new things (1 Cor. 13:12) and have work to do (Rev. 22:3).

But maybe the most telling details are the ones Jesus gave his closest friends at their last meal together the night before he died:

> Do not let your hearts be troubled. You believe in God. Believe in me also. There are many rooms in my Father's house. If this were not true, would I have told you that I am going

there? Would I have told you that I would prepare a place for you there? If I go and do that, I will come back. And I will take you to be with me. Then you will also be where I am. You know the way to the place where I am going. (John 14:1–4)

We fear loss because we view death through one lens—ours. We don't view it through Jesus's lens, which is gain. For all we know, heaven is as complex and dynamic as earth is, minus all the crap that hurts. Loss hurts. There's no way around that. We miss the people and the relationships that are no longer immediately within our grasp. But there is hope. If that weren't true, Jesus wouldn't have said it was. Through him, we have access to an afterlife that far exceeds our expectations. Paul said, "For me, life finds all its meaning in Christ." But "death also has its benefits" (Phil. 1:21). When people die, it's OK to cry. It's OK to be angry. It's OK to raise your fist and tell God it isn't fair. Jesus understands. Remember, Jesus wept when he saw Lazarus's sisters and the other mourners grieving his passing (John 11:35). I believe Jesus's tears had more to do with how sad he felt for the onlookers. He knew he was about to raise Lazarus back to life. He wasn't crying for the loss but for the pain that it had caused the ones he loved.

Jesus had compassion for Lazarus's loved ones. True, no death is outside of God's permission. And Jesus delayed coming to Lazarus and healing him before he died. But that doesn't mean Jesus didn't care. That doesn't mean he reacted to Lazarus's sickness casually.

Lamentations 3:33 says, "He doesn't want to bring pain or suffering to anyone." Sometimes the plans of God require momentary discomfort or pain (suffering) to bring about the bigger miracle or to satisfy the greater good.

But our suffering doesn't bring him joy. He's not zapping us and watching us writhe. No, Jesus shares in our pain. When we cry, he cries with us.[1]

We'll probably never *not* fear loss. At least I won't. I embrace that dread as a sign that I'm blessed enough to love people I'd be devastated to lose. But I also won't allow that fear to make me suffer. Instead, I try to view death and loss through Jesus's lens. There's a lot I don't understand about it, but what I do know is this: death is not the end if we have hope in Jesus as our Savior; it's the beginning of life as God meant us to know it.

We've talked about several types of fear. Vague fears we aren't likely to be confronted with unless we go in search of them—like sharks. Weird phobias that make our skin crawl—like loose hair. The dread of the unknown—such as pandemics, the future of our country, and loss. But there's one other fear I think many of us struggle with that we don't normally talk about. That's the fear of offering forgiveness.

I know that sounds counterintuitive. Why would we be fearful to forgive? Being afraid to offer absolution doesn't seem like the hard part. Being so mad at your offender that you could explode through a brick wall like She-Hulk does. But if you think about it, so much of our unforgiveness is rooted in fear.

When someone wrongs us, we feel like they owe us something. They're in debt to us. Think about it. Your friends don't invite you to the girls' night out? You feel they owe you better friendship. Your spouse spends too much time on the golf course? You feel they owe you more time. Your pastor says something from the pulpit you disagree with? You feel they owe you a different opinion. That's what it comes down to: we didn't get what we want, so we're owed what we want.

Don't get me wrong. Not all anger and hurt feelings are trivial. People can wound us. And I mean *really* hurt us. I've hurt more in the last year than I can ever remember hurting before. And sometimes, they really do owe us better, more, different. Being wronged is not the part we need to work on. It's OK to feel angry, mad, indignant rage. But it's not OK to hang on to it.

But we do! And I think we hang on to unforgiveness out of fear.

Over time, unforgiveness causes us more suffering than just about any other source of suffering we go through. Unforgiveness leaves us feeling anxious, isolated, and restless. Unforgiveness can even make us physically sick. "Chronic anger puts you into a fight-or-flight mode, which results in numerous changes in heart rate, blood pressure, and immune response. Those changes, then, increase the risk of depression, heart disease, and diabetes, among other conditions."[2]

I'm guessing you've already heard how unforgiveness needlessly ties you to the person you haven't forgiven, weighing you down. And you've also probably heard that if you want to be forgiven, you must first forgive those you hold resentment toward. But maybe you haven't heard that when it comes to forgiveness, you don't have to be afraid.

You don't have to be afraid that forgiveness means you have to allow that person to come back into your life. You don't. You don't even have to speak to them ever again. Heck, you don't even have to *tell them* you forgive them. Although,

I think that's an incredibly powerful and empowering act. You don't have to reestablish that relationship on the same terms. It's OK to move that relationship to the periphery or even to end it.

God doesn't say, "Thou shalt be nice to everyone!" He doesn't even say we have to like everyone. Instead, his commandment is simply to love your neighbor as yourself. Love, in this instance, means releasing them from the "debt" you believe they owe you.

Sometimes you'll have to forgive someone again and again for the same offense. That's OK. It doesn't mean you're bad at forgiveness. It means you're human. There will be resentments that pop back up in your heart out of nowhere, and you'll have to forgive that person all over again.

Sometimes after forgiveness comes a pause in the relationship. Forgiving someone doesn't mean you have to act like nothing happened. It doesn't make everything OK between the two of you. As I've said, forgiveness cancels debt. What it doesn't do is erase what happened. There are natural consequences to people's actions. And it's OK to press pause on a relationship until the sting of the injury has lessened.

Ephesians 4:32 says, "Be kind and tender to one another. Forgive one another, just as God forgave you because of what Christ has done." God has forgiven us for more than we're even aware of. The kind of grace he offers us doesn't compute because we're not capable of it. Because he really does forgive and forget. He doesn't need relational distance from us. In fact, some of my most intimate moments with God have been after repentance. No, we can't forgive like God can. But we do have the opportunity to express our deep gratitude to him by offering forgiveness to his people.

I'm willing to bet that if the honest-to-goodness peace of God were available for purchase at Target on Black Friday, we'd be sliding our carts around the aisles on two wheels. But we don't have to purchase the peace of God. Jesus already did that. Don't allow the struggle of fear—the fear of sharks, the fear of the unknown, the fear of forgiveness—to steal your potential for peace.

It's a peace Jesus purposefully traded his life to give us.

8

Trees of Life

Hope that is put off makes one sick at heart.
But a desire that is met is like a tree of life.

Proverbs 13:12

I've always wanted to go to culinary school. It might seem ironic to you that a girl with an eating disorder grew up with a passion for cooking, but I didn't make me—God did. That's one of the many inherent contradictions in life that I chalk up to God's quirky sense of humor.

I would absolutely adore going on a cooking tour through Italy. I mean, can you imagine? Worn, well-loved kitchens with terra-cotta tile, fresh herbs in clay pots, and hearths with open flames for cooking in Dutch ovens. Tasting chocolates in Turin, drinking coffee in Trieste, and picking lemons off the Amalfi coast. A girl can dream, right?

And you might say, "Landra, your dad is Ed Young! He's a bestselling author. He can afford to send you to Italy." Well, yes, he can, but that's not how it works in my family. My parents are the most generous people you'll ever meet, but they're still good parents. They don't hand out free trips to Italy. And they shouldn't. I've learned how to work hard, spend cautiously, and save because I've had to. I hope to pass those same character traits along to my kids. I don't think they can be taught any other way.

But a girl can dream.

I dreamed all the time growing up. I dreamed of leading a church like my mom and dad. I dreamed of having an exciting, loving marriage like my parents have. I dreamed of being a mother. I dreamed of raising my kids to love God first. I dreamed of a lot of things that have actually happened. And I am deeply thankful.

But what happens to us when we get older? We get married, we have families, we get jobs. And for many of us, we stop dreaming. Sure, we have goals—lose five pounds, go on one vacation a year, and keep a certain amount in our savings accounts. But they don't have the same almost magical and whimsical feeling that dreams do. In fact, I'm willing to bet that many of us have lost the ability to dream at all. Or maybe it's not that we can't; we just don't. Somewhere along the journey of life, we stop dreaming.

I think the main difference between a dream and a goal is that a goal is something we work toward and a dream is something we don't have the guts (or energy) to work toward. It's true! If I really wanted to go on a cooking tour of Italy, I'd create a little savings account just for that purpose. I'd do side jobs or speaking engagements and put that money away to realize my dream. But I don't. I just sort of hope that it falls into my lap.

If you are honest about your dreams, you'd probably say the same thing. You dream of starting your own business, you dream of leaving an abusive relationship, you dream of moving away on your own. You dream of saving money, of a new job, of a family of your own. You dream of a better life. But you don't do anything about your dreams, living as if you either expect them not to happen at all or you expect them to happen on their own.

I think we've stopped pursuing our dreams because we're afraid. Not the kind of fear we talked about in the previous chapter. This emotion is fear's evil cousin—doubt. We're afraid that if we try, we may fail at it. We're afraid of how different life might be if we pursue our dreams and they actually *do* come true. We're afraid if we admit our dreams out loud, other people may judge us or laugh at us. Instead of our dreams inspiring us, our dreams fill us with doubt.

I get the idea of scary dreams. I have horrible dreams about LeeBeth a lot right now. In one in particular, I somehow know that she's one literal step away from death. She's struggling to keep her feet in place, but they're being pulled, tugged in the direction of danger. I'm just standing there, looking at her. And as she's slipping away, I don't tell her how much I love her. I don't tell her to go to the hospital. I don't say a word. I know I want to save her, but I also know that I can't. So I just stand and watch as she takes that final step into despair and death, without saying a single word.

It doesn't require a Joseph-level dream interpreter to figure that one out. I obviously have a lot of guilt in connection to LeeBeth's death. It's unmerited, of course. But the thing about guilt is that it can be completely baseless and still consume you. Ultimately, LeeBeth was a grown woman who made her own choices. I was there for her the best way I knew how to be. But it wasn't enough. She knew she was loved by her family and by God, and I guess that's more than a lot of people can say about loved ones who have died.

LeeBeth had dreams too. You've already heard the biggest—to be a wife and mother. She took every step she could to realize those dreams. She was beautiful. She took care of herself (until the binge drinking started). She worked hard. She was smart and funny. She took chances, going on dates and being vulnerable with people. From my perspective, Lee-Beth did everything she could to make those dreams come true. But they never did.

Why?

Why did my dream of having a family come true and LeeBeth's didn't? I think the process of wrestling with this question and others like it explains why we stop dreaming when we become adults. There is no satisfactory answer. Some people see their dreams fulfilled and others don't. So we decide that instead of having a dream go unrealized, we'd rather not dream at all.

Let's look at what the Bible has to say about our dreams:

> Hope that is put off makes one sick at heart.
>   But a desire that is met is like a tree of life. (Prov. 13:12)

Hope "put off" can be illustrated by a number of common circumstances. It can be a long struggle with infertility. It can be a job search that feels like constant rejection. It can be seasons of being single when it feels like everyone around you has a partner. It can be a house hunt that feels like a never-ending roller coaster.

But hope "put off" for too long can lead us into dark emotional territory if we're not careful. It can lead us into despair.[1] Despair is one of the most dangerous human conditions. I heard someone say once that people who take their own lives aren't just depressed—they're in despair. Despair is the absence of all hope. Despair means we can't see any way that life could get any better for us. When our hope is put off too long, it's a struggle of suffering that blinds us to all other things that are true and good in our lives.

The Good News Translation of the first part of Proverbs 13:12 says, "When hope is crushed, the heart is crushed." When we wait for what we determine to be a good thing for so long that the desire and expectation turn to hopelessness, we can become spiritually dried up, leaving us horrendously vulnerable to the enemy's attacks.[2] Solomon is basically saying that any time we don't get what we want when we want it, we become weak, hopeless, and at-risk for emotions that lead us to want to take our own lives.

That sounds a little dramatic. I mean, that can't be right, can it? If our dreams are just a little later than we'd like, we can wait. We're grown-ups. We're professional wait-ers. But I think the problem is that when our dreams aren't realized on our timetable or when we think is "best" for us, we assume God is withholding from us. Or we assume we're not worthy of our dreams—not smart enough, wealthy enough, or good enough.

If we've waited but still don't see a dream fulfilled, we make up our minds that it's never going to happen for us. And you know what? Maybe it won't. We may never get married. We may never get a baby. We may never get our own business. We may never get promoted. We may never get our parents' approval. We may never get healing. We may never get to see our loved one restored or walking with God. We may never get our version of our dreams.

Those dashed hopes grieve our spirits. And not just on an emotional level but on a chemical level too. When our bodies experience feelings of hopefulness, our hormone levels change. In an article titled "The Anatomy of Hope," author and scientist Jerome Groopman writes, "Belief and expectation—the key elements of hope—can block pain by releasing the brain's endorphins and enkephalins, mimicking the effects of morphine. In some cases, hope can also have important effects on fundamental physiological processes like respiration, circulation and motor function."[3] The reason people say "hope heals" is because, according to science, it actually can. It's not just a spiritual experience but also a physical one.

So is it any wonder that when those feelings (and chemicals) of hopefulness are gone, we feel such defeat and misery? The higher our expectations, the greater our frustrations when our dreams aren't realized.

Let me ask you a question: Have you ever made one of your kids' dreams come true? It doesn't always turn out as expected, does it? Have you ever watched those videos parents post of surprising their kids with a trip to Disney? But instead of bursting into applause and cheers of glee, the kids just kind of look at one another and shrug in response. It's funny to watch, but I wonder how many times I've done that. How many times has God made my dreams come true and I've shrugged in response? Not literally, but emotionally? How many dreams am I living right now that I fail to recognize?

I have a husband who loves me.

I have children who are healthy.

I'm walking in healing from an eating disorder.

My loved ones know Jesus.

I am making a living at a church whose mission lines up with my passions.

Gosh, even just typing that, I am struck with the life I'm living right now. I'm literally living the dream. My dreams. Yes, I am thankful for all these gifts from God, but do I walk away from the dreams long enough to say, "Thank you, God! You are the best God in the entire world!" and hug him and then go back and enjoy my realized dreams with a happy and grateful heart?

Friend, if you're longing for something right now, if you're heartsick because your hopes have been delayed, I ask you to pause and consider the dreams you are currently living out. Learning to show daily and intentional thankfulness is the *best* medicine for heartsickness. Don't allow what you don't have to become more important than what you do have. This is a mindset I have to cling to anytime I become restless in waiting (which is often).

While getting what we dream for feels incredible, the chase of what we want can lead us into unhealthy, messy cycles. The obsessive nature our pursuits take on can even be called *sin*.

When I got pregnant with Sterling, I had a close friend who had just completed her second unsuccessful round of intrauterine insemination (IUI) treatments. I was terrified to tell her. Getting pregnant was her dream. She'd invested time, money, and thousands of prayers to become pregnant.

Then here I was, pregnant as soon as Brad and I started trying. Finally, I knew I couldn't put it off any longer. People knew. I could only pass off my growing bump as a food baby for so long.

"I'm so sorry to tell you this," I said, "but I'm pregnant."

She shot up out of her chair like a rocket. "Landra!" she squealed. "I am *so* happy for you!"

Her response was selflessly generous. When she asked me why I prefaced my news with an apology, I said, "I want to be sensitive to you. I feel guilty."

She looked at me sideways. "Landra, you being pregnant doesn't make me *less* pregnant."

What she said made me think. Someone else's success doesn't make me less successful. Someone else's win doesn't make me a loser. Someone else's dreams coming true doesn't make me less likely to have my dreams come true.

But in the moment, that's how it can feel. When someone else gets what they want, it can be a stark reminder that we've yet to get what we want. How my first book performed is an example. I see all these successful authors my age in my season of life, and I'm tempted to think, *What do they have that I lack? What am I doing wrong?* Then I worry I'm pursuing the wrong things and that maybe my dreams are somehow wrong or misguided.

This reaction of heartsickness is best dosed by behaving just like my sweet friend did—celebrating the dreams of others. We're a big "girl boss" society on the surface, but how many of us truly cheer for, pray for, and support the dreams of our friends and contemporaries? How many of us are behind the scenes and in the trenches with one another? Does someone else's success make us feel less successful? And look—I've been there. This is a struggle that's real for me today. It's *hard* to move your heart in the direction of celebration when all you're feeling is disappointment and shame.

You can't make your heart feel anything, but you can train it. Following are some suggestions for how to do that:

Write notes of encouragement and mean them.

Speak highly of others when it doesn't benefit you.

Celebrate others' wins publicly.

Pray for them privately.

Little by little, your heart will follow your actions. And instead of struggling with a sick heart when someone else gets what you want, you're able to genuinely be glad for them.

No one likes to wait. No one. I will drive to a completely different Starbucks just to avoid the long line of another. Have I saved time? No, but I'm not sitting in a car, waiting, either. This isn't a new problem. It's actually one we read about in some of the earliest chapters of the Old Testament.

Esau and Jacob were twins born into rivalry. Even before their birth, God prophesied over their mother, Rebekah:

Two nations are in your body.
  Two tribes that are now inside you will be separated.
One nation will be stronger than the other.
  The older son will serve the younger one. (Gen. 25:23)

To say the boys were born into a dysfunctional family dynamic would be an understatement. Isaac (their father) favored Esau, who was the older brother and a hunter—a guy's guy—but Rebekah preferred Jacob, who was a mama's boy and didn't like to leave home. Instead of being decent parents, Isaac and Rebekah pitted the brothers against each other. It became clear early on that Jacob desperately dreamed of receiving his father's blessing and would try to gain it by any means necessary.

When Isaac was old and losing his vision, Rebekah devised an elaborate plan for Jacob to receive the birthright blessing belonging to his older brother, Esau. By deceiving Isaac with a (to her credit, creative) disguise, Jacob received the blessing that was rightfully his brother's. When Esau discovered the ruse, he yelled bitterly, "Bless me! Bless me too, my father!" (Gen. 27:34).

But there are no backsies in birthright blessings. Isaac couldn't revoke what he'd given to Jacob, so he had to give Esau a lesser blessing. In Genesis 27:41 we're told that Esau was angry with Jacob. To which we say, *Duh*. But that anger quickly turned into a murderous rage. Esau vowed to get revenge by killing his brother. When Rebekah heard of his plan, she sent Jacob to live with her brother until Esau had "forgotten" what Jacob had done to him (v. 45). (For me, that would have been *never*-thirty.)

We hear this story about Jacob and think, *What a terrible guy. How selfish and shady. He's bad.* But then, how often do we seek someone else's blessings for our own lives? I'm cringing as I type this because I'm guilty of it too. It's easy for us to sit back and think, *Gosh, they've got it made. Why are they doing so much better than I am? Why do they have so much more than I do?* Once we're stuck in the cycle of the comparison trap, it's a very thankless climb out.

When what we want becomes more important than how we get it, we can almost guarantee sin is at play. In fact, when what we want becomes more important than who we want it from, it's called idolatry.

How do we avoid the suffering of heartsickness? How do we avoid idolizing our dreams over our dream giver? Through patience and positioning.

Patience is maybe my least favorite word. I grew up hearing people tease, "Don't ask God for patience," meaning this spiritual discipline is one of the *least* fun to practice. But in order to avoid the suffering of heartsickness, we have to learn patience. We can start by reframing what it means to wait. Instead of treading water emotionally, climb on the raft of God's assurances and rest in his unfailing promises. Commit useful, hopeful Scripture to memory such as the following verses:

The LORD will fight for you. Just be still. (Exod. 14:14)

> Wait for the LORD.
> > Be strong and don't lose hope.
> Wait for the LORD. (Ps. 27:14)

We hope for what we don't have yet. So we are patient as we wait for it. (Rom. 8:25)

When you hope, be joyful. When you suffer, be patient. When you pray, be faithful. (Rom. 12:12)

The Lord is not slow to keep his promise. He is not slow in the way some people understand it. Instead, he is patient with you. He doesn't want anyone to be destroyed. Instead, he wants all people to turn away from their sins. (2 Pet. 3:9)

Reframe waiting patiently as an opportunity to grow your trust and dependence on God. It may not be a total blast, but character-building experiences rarely are. And remember, God isn't interested in making us happy; he's interested in making us his. Our deferred hopes can lead us to intimate places in our relationship with God that we'd never have reached if he were merely a cosmic vending machine in the sky, dispensing our dreams at our will.

The other way we can avoid the suffering of heartsickness is by positioning—or repositioning—our dreams. If I were to ask you, "Where do you put your hope? Where do you put your faith?" I seriously doubt you'd say, "In getting married." "In being a professional speaker." "In having a bestseller." "In being thin." "In having a baby boy." And yet, the way our minds work when we don't get those desires and longings, it's as if we have no hope at all. It's as if the things we want become the source of our hope—and not God.

If we confess Jesus to be our hope and our Savior, then we should let him give us hope and save us. The truth is God knows that we need him more than anything else in our lives. And sometimes the process of waiting for what we want is a simple reminder from him that *he* is our safe place and refuge. He is our joy. He is our peace. God and God alone can meet our needs and satisfy us.

It's OK to want something. In fact, God wants us to dream. He even wants us to talk about our dreams. Proverbs 16:1–3 says:

> People make plans in their hearts.
>   But the LORD puts the correct answer on their tongues.
> Everything a person does might seem pure to them.
>   But the LORD knows why they do what they do.

Commit to the LORD everything you do.
Then he will make your plans succeed.

We make plans, yes. But God lets us know what to ask for. In other words, your dreams are very likely *from* God. What you're asking for, he wants to give you. If your intentions are pure, the Bible promises that if you commit or hand over your dreams to him, you will succeed.

Which brings us to the second half of a verse we looked at earlier:

Hope that is put off makes one sick at heart.
But a desire that is met is like a tree of life. (Prov. 13:12)

A longing fulfilled is a renewal. It's refreshing. It's new life. When our dreams come true, when our prayers are answered, our soul experiences revival. Solomon reiterates in verse 19, "A desire that is met is like something that tastes sweet."[4]

If you know anything about God, you know it's his good pleasure to give to his children. He's our parent—our heavenly Father—and if you know any parents, you know there's nothing more exciting to them than giving their kids something they want. So if you're dreaming of or longing for something that hasn't yet come to pass, keep on hoping.

Before LeeBeth got sick for the last time, my hopes were way, way up that she would stay in recovery from her addiction. I was pouring into her, encouraging her, and talking to her every chance she would give me. In fact, Sterling was *super* into FaceTime during this period, and she and LeeBeth started having FaceTime dates. I can't tell you how glad it made my heart to watch them connect. LeeBeth had a relationship with Sterling that no one else did.

When she got sick again, those hopes were crushed. Looking back, I was so angry with God. I was so angry with Lee-Beth. Why would God allow her a special place in Sterling's heart just to take it away?

But now, in light of losing LeeBeth, every second Sterling got to engage with her is an invaluable gift that I am deeply thankful for.

Don't stop dreaming because you've tried and failed.

Don't stop dreaming because the wait seems long.

Don't stop dreaming because someone else got your dream before you did.

Don't stop dreaming because it's a risk.

Dreaming and hoping may make us vulnerable to disappointment, but Christ is "a strong and trustworthy anchor for our souls" (Heb. 6:19 NLT). When our hope rests only in him, we can rest in the security of his many promises.

Do I regret having hope in LeeBeth's recovery and healing? No. I didn't get what I hoped for or dreamed of, but Sterling *did* get moments with her aunt that, in the absence of hope, would never have happened.

9

I Have an Opinion,
Your Honor

Do not judge other people. Then you will not be judged.

Matthew 7:1

Few things can top the immediate panic I feel whenever I see flashing blue lights in my rearview mirror. Can you relate? It doesn't matter if I'm going five under the speed limit with my hands at ten and two. My immediate reaction is either *I hope they're after someone else* or *Oh, crap. What did I do?*

One Sunday morning I was driving down the Dallas tollway. If you're at all familiar with the area, you know that drivers on the Dallas tollway operate under an unspoken understanding that we will all speed, but we'll all speed together. That way, it doesn't look like any of us are speeding.

There I was, listening to my worship music and having honestly a pretty powerful spiritual moment.

And then I saw them—flashing blue lights. I had no idea what I could possibly have been doing wrong, but I pulled over.

"Ma'am," the cop said, "do you have any idea how fast you were going?"

I did not.

"You were traveling twenty miles per hour over the speed limit," he informed me.

I guess I was just really in the presence of God, y'all. Because I had no idea I was going that fast. Believe it or not, the police officer did *not* care that I had been in the middle of a Kari Jobe classic, just inches from the throne. He gave me a ticket—a super-expensive ticket.

I couldn't decide which was worse—getting ticketed or having to tell Brad about it. This was not a good day. In fact, when I look back on it, one memory stands out more than any of the others. I will never forget the expression on the cop's face when I rolled down my window to speak to him. It was a look of pure, unadulterated judgment.

Have you ever been looked at that way? It's a detached look, a surmising one. It makes you feel about three inches tall. But that wasn't the first time I'd been judged. Far from it.

As I've mentioned, when I was in high school, there was a huge news story about my family. This wasn't just small-time gossip on the local Facebook groups. This was the news on television. Basically, it was a story about how my parents chose to spend their money. Which is pretty incredible if you think about it. We don't see many indicting news stories about how celebrities spend their money. No, we put them on episodes of *MTV Cribs* and congratulate them. Anyway, the story was slathered in lies and perpetuated by some of our closest friends and members of the church staff.

The judgment felt so heavy that I wore it like a ball and chain, lugging it around with me wherever I went. And this wasn't a situation where I was imagining the whispers and stares—it was all real.

Judgment like that can isolate you. It separates you from others. On one hand, you're not sure who you can trust. On the other, there aren't a whole lot of people offering.

In a word, being judged *sucks*. When we deserve it, it sucks. And when we don't deserve it, it sucks.

In the Christian world, our go-to verse about judgment is Matthew 7:1: "Do not judge other people. Then you will not be judged." You may have memorized it as "Judge not, that you be not judged" (NKJV).

I've never considered myself a judgmental person. But does anyone? Think about it. How many people do you meet that say, "Hey, and just so you know, I'm super judgmental."

No one readily admits to being judgmental when we all low-key are. I know I am. I remember when my mom bought me the book *Redeeming Love* by Francine Rivers. You know how they say to never judge a book by its cover? Well, that's exactly what I did. I took one look at the outdated, 1990s special and said, "Nope. I don't want to read that." I literally judged a book by its cover. But my mom insisted, and I'm so thankful she did. *Redeeming Love* still ranks high in my favorite books of all time.

I think judgmentalism is part of human nature. We all have a sense of right and wrong. It's one of the very first lessons we learn. At the very least, we all have ideas about how things *should* be done. Think about it—government, parenting, church, marriage, school, dating, not dating. We all have an idea about the correct way to go about life. And when someone's views or ideas or beliefs are different from ours? It's hard not to judge them.

Let me give you an example. I follow someone on social media I used to go to school with. She's absolutely stunning. Somehow, she's prettier now after four kids and two decades than she was when we grew up together. I know this because she posts pictures and stories of herself multiple times a day. I just opened Instagram and counted. In the last week, she's posted ten photos. She is in every single one of them. And not just her, but her assets as well. And I'm not talking about cars and houses. I'm talking about her body, dang near all of it.

For the longest time, every time she posted something it would annoy me. I'd find myself rolling my eyes and shaking my head. *She's so thirsty for attention*, I would think to myself. *Why doesn't she respect herself more? She has kids! One day her kids are going to grow up and see these posts!*

I shared my thoughts with my sister Laurie. Fully expecting her to jump on the bandwagon with me, I didn't even know what to say when she said, "Landra. Don't you think that's a little bit judgmental?"

No! I'm not being judgmental. I'm being right!

But that's what it's about, isn't it? When we think we're right, we can't imagine another possibility or perspective. Which is at the core of judgmentalism.

Here's a better example from the Bible. In John 4, Jesus had one of the most famous interactions in all of the New Testament. In those days, Samaritans were considered "dogs" or "half-breeds" and were judged as unclean by full-blooded Jews.

Jesus was traveling through a Samaritan town and stopped at one of Jacob's wells for a drink. While at the well, he asked a Samaritan woman for some water. She said to him, "'You are a Jew. I am a Samaritan woman. How can you ask me for a drink?' She said this because Jews don't have anything to do with Samaritans" (v. 9). I don't know if she was just curious or if the Samaritan woman was doing a little judging of her own. But she begins her conversation with Jesus by calling him out for his social faux pas. I kind of love her for that.

Jesus replied, "You do not know what God's gift is. And you do not know who is asking you for a drink. If you did, you would have asked him. He would have given you living water" (v. 10).

Our well-dweller doesn't understand Jesus's analogy. I doubt you or I would have either. Jesus liked to talk in riddles. Why? I don't know. Probably because it caused the people he was talking with to ask questions. And that's exactly what the Samaritan woman did.

> "Sir," the woman said, "you don't have anything to get water with. The well is deep. Where can you get this living water? Our father Jacob gave us the well. He drank from it himself. So did his sons and his livestock. Are you more important than he is?"
>
> Jesus answered, "Everyone who drinks this water will be thirsty again. But anyone who drinks the water I give them will never be thirsty. In fact, the water I give them will become a spring of water in them. It will flow up into eternal life." (vv. 11–14)

Jesus went on to tell her that she should get her husband and let him drink. The woman responded by telling Jesus that she did not have a husband. What Jesus says next may be the most overlooked example of how Christ followers should react when we disagree with someone else's choices and lifestyle. He states the facts: "You are right when you say you have no husband. The fact is, you have had five husbands. And the man you live with now is not your husband. What you have just said is very true" (vv. 17–18).

That was it. That was what Jesus said to her, a woman who clearly needed to examine her life choices. Did you see any opinion or assumptions mingled with Jesus's response to her? Did you see any advice? No, the only thing Jesus adds is that, oh, and by the way, I am the Messiah you've been waiting for.

And the illustration of how not to judge was laid out for us: Facts + Jesus = Increased awareness of God's grace.

That's it! No indictment. No shaming. No reminders of what's right and wrong. No guilt trips. No lectures. No soapbox.

Speaking of soapboxes.

Facebook is the world's most popular social media platform with over 2.89 billion *active* users.[1] I'm not going to start lambasting social media or even Facebook right now. I see a lot of good come out of platforms like these—especially since the pandemic. When used in a healthy way, social media is awesome. It's helpful. It's great for marketing, for getting outfit or home décor ideas, and for staying connected to current culture and news.

However, we all know it's also a cesspool for judgment. There are tons of stories shared on social media that may be loosely based on facts but are mostly weighted down by bias and emotion. People find these platforms to be a comfortable place to assess politicians and celebrities, but just as natural a place to judge friends, family, and neighbors.

Have you ever scrolled through your newsfeed during election season? Good gracious. Nothing makes you lose faith in the future of humanity quite like the mudslinging done online in the name of politics. I've seen people I know personally, who are otherwise balanced and wise, use poor filters from time to time when they're on social media.

The result is that we can find ourselves judging people we don't even know . . . *and* many people we know and love.

Not long ago, there was a huge debate in my local community about a proposed Hindu temple on a few acres of land right in the middle of the suburbs. The land was not zoned for a temple, so a vote was coming before the county commissioners for approval. The temple's plans were elaborate and massive—including a few priest houses, decorative spires, and other architectural details that did not at all blend with its proposed surroundings (subdivision-type housing).

Man oh man, you better believe activists on both sides wielded their keyboards in their pursuit of defending their stance. Those in favor of the temple argued that people have a right to religious freedom and that landowners also have the right to build whatever they want on land they've legally purchased or obtained. Those against the temple argued that a structure of that size and design would be an eyesore that would lower home values in the area as well as cause traffic congestion and noise.

It turned into the very definition of a *mess*.

The vote pitted even those with profound spiritual convictions against one another. Some were very passionate about it and others were indecisive. I watched online as people started to question the moral character of those they had known for years because of their stance on this one, single measure. It ruined relationships and tarnished reputations. Over what? A piece of land that almost every person commenting had no vested interest in.

Instead of stating the facts, "Bob the commissioner is voting in favor of the Hindu temple, and I disagree with his choice," it turned into "Bob is voting for the Hindu temple. He has to be pocketing money from that builder. You know, reelection is right around the corner. He's just trying to make everybody happy. I heard he's not even going to church anymore. He's such a sellout."

This is what happens when people rush to judge others and share their opinions. But there's a difference between stating facts and making assumptions. Take my friend's Instagram posts for example. The *facts* are that she posts a ton of pictures of herself. My *assumption* was that she did it for attention. But what if I'm wrong? What if she posts without even considering that her image will turn heads?

We've all heard the saying, "Assuming will make an *ass* out of *you* and *me*." (If you don't like me using the word *ass*, check out the King James Version of the Bible!) Assuming is what people did over two thousand years ago, and we are still assuming and speculating today.

You might be reading this and thinking, *Landra, I'm not one of* those *people. I don't get on social media and air out my dirty opinion of others. I keep my judgments and assumptions to myself.* But that's even more dangerous! At least the people blabbing on Facebook aren't ruminating on their opinions. And if you aren't familiar with what it means to ruminate, let me explain it to you. (Disclaimer: I might have grown up in Texas, but I don't know anything about cows. I had to google what *ruminate* means, and let me tell you, it's disgusting.)

A cow's stomach has four compartments. The first is the rumen where their food begins to be broken down. But a cow's food can be regurgitated so that it can chew on the cud before swallowing it again. That's where the term *ruminate* comes from. And honestly, it's just as gross when we ruminate on our own assumptions.

Listen, I'm so guilty of this! I am preaching to myself here. Someone posts something cryptic on their Instagram? I will be scrolling their grid for an hour looking for clues to support whatever assumption I'm making. I hear of a marriage that's fallen apart? I am on their profile trying to figure out where and when it all went wrong. But this isn't at all the model for judgment that Jesus set. In fact, this type of judgment is insidious. It erodes relationships and leads to a type of suffering that can only be described by people who have experienced it.

It's human nature, though, isn't it? To want to *know.* To want the dirt. Once we have what we think are the facts, we don't let it drop there. We assign a moral judgment to the situation and its parties. We assign blame and treat people accordingly. When you think about it, we put ourselves on equal footing with God—the judge and the jury and the enforcer of the punishment.

I'm pretty sure (certain) that Jesus is disgusted with our judgment of his brothers and sisters.

How do we stop judging others? We deal with our judgmental thoughts as soon as we notice them. When we feel our mental gavel start to rise and fall, we stop it. We state the facts and only the facts about a given situation. After that, we move on and give our minds some rest. We focus our attention back on the moment and away from what caused the judgment. Simply practicing letting judgments pass without acting on them, sharing them, or believing them will lessen the power they have over our mood and behavior. With time, we'll start to notice them immediately and say, "That's just a judgment," and go on with our day.

One way to reframe our opinions of others is to recognize that we all value different things. Just because someone's values vary from our own doesn't mean they're bad people. It just means that they have different priorities.

Let me tell you a story to illustrate. It's time for a new TV for the house. You've been scoping out those Black Friday deals online. You've got a budget though, so you narrow it down to one perfect TV. It's off-brand, but the reviews are great. You're already pregaming the midnight wait in line with coffee when your spouse sends you a screenshot of a totally different TV. A TV that's double your budget.

Which emoji should I use to respond? you think. *The skull? The one that's throwing up? Ohhhh, I know. The red-faced emoji that's cussing.*

I know, I know. We'd all want to tell our partners to shove their screenshot straight into their recently deleted folder. But before you rush to judgment and start sharing your feelings about it, take a minute to state the facts to yourself. Remove the emotion from the situation and evaluate what's *true*. You know that above all else, your spouse values *quality* over all other factors when it comes to making purchases. You are someone who prioritizes value; you'll buy any brand TV on sale as long as it has good reviews.

What you have isn't a difference in moral character—it's a difference in value systems. One isn't right or wrong; it's just different.

Why is this so hard for us to see? I think the answer has to do with Matthew 7:1: "Do not judge other people." Why are we not to judge others? Because that's not what we were created to do. James 4:12 tells us, "There is only one Law-giver and Judge. He is the God who is able to save life or destroy it. But who are you to judge your neighbor?" The Bible tells us in the simplest, easiest terms possible that we aren't meant to judge others. Only God can do that. Why? Because we can't see their hearts or motives. What we see are the external contributing factors to a person's words or actions, which are almost always colored by our emotions and assumptions.

Now, there is a time and a place and a method for pointing out another believer's sin out of love and concern. It's in our attitude and our approach. But that's not what I'm talking about here. This is about the rush to judgment. Making assumptions. The words we fling over social media and the things we whisper behind closed doors that eviscerate reputations and relationships.

If you've been on the receiving end of assumptions, which I'm sure we all have at some point, you understand the suffering of being the judged. If you've done something that merits judgment, the opinions of others serve only to heap coals on your head. If you haven't done something that merits judgment, the unfounded opinions of others serve only to isolate and alienate you, not to mention erase your trust and hope in humanity. Either way, the suffering is relentless.

Why? Because the result of judgment is almost never what it should be—an increased awareness of God's grace. Because the only effective judgment isn't judgment at all—it's love. Think about it.

If you've been judged before or you're being judged for something right now, I want to pause here and tell you that I'm sorry. There isn't a man or woman on this earth without sin. You're no better or worse than anyone else. Jesus died for you. He did. He loves you and wants you just as much as he loves and wants the squeaky-clean members of society (of which, to be clear, there are none). If you're in a situation you know you shouldn't be in, get out. If you're involved in a sinful relationship, end it. If you're doing wrong, stop. While there are natural consequences to sin, there is always grace. So much grace. Run from the behaviors that are hurting you and inviting judgment.

Maybe you judge your younger sibling because they're spoiled and catered to. Maybe you judge your boss because you've got a better degree or more experience. Maybe you judge your neighbors because their kids are always wild and screaming. Maybe you judge the lady at church whose husband left her. Maybe she even cheated, so from your perspective, she deserved it. Maybe, like me, you judge your friend on Instagram for oversharing. For all of us, I say the same thing: if you're judging someone, stop. If you're in a relationship where the two of you just sit around and judge people, end it. If getting on social media turns you into Judge Judy, delete it.

A sin is a sin is a sin is a sin. And Jesus told us plain as day that we are *not* to judge one another.

But Landra, you might say. *My father-in-law is abusive. My pastor was unfaithful. My sister is toxic.* All of these things may be true. And it's going to be incredibly hard not to be judgmental. I would encourage you to bring these situations before God (and to others if needed). Ask God to heal the parts of you wounded by the actions of others. Then ask him to remove any judgment from your heart. If you find yourself in the position of needing to speak truth to someone, examine your heart, your attitude, and your posture first. There's a difference between judgment and accountability.

The Bible tells us that before we act to remove the speck of sawdust from someone else's eye, we first have to take out the plank from our own eye (Matt. 7:5). In other words, before you confront someone regarding their sin, you need to do some work on yourself first. You have to make sure your words, thoughts, and actions toward this person are wholesome and pure. Approach them in love, without judgment; that's the only way to move them closer to God. Which should above all things be our ultimate goal as believers.

For example, when I was struggling with my eating disorder, there was no shortage of people who noticed. In fact, it was as if every single person I encountered all day long was judging me and confronting me. Certain relationships were reduced to little more than calling me out for how I looked. Looking back, I can see that people were frustrated. They were scared. But at the time, the last people I wanted to talk to were the ones sitting in constant judgment of me.

But then there was my sister Laurie. Laurie had this way about her that was different. She made a point to talk to me about things unrelated to my sin. She was one of the only people to treat me like I was still *Landra*. That didn't mean she didn't ask me tough questions. She did. But that wasn't the basis of our relationship. The way she treated me made it clear that she loved and valued me, despite what I was going through and despite what I had done.

Laurie was also extremely patient with me. I lied to her many times about how I was doing, but she was always willing to forgive me when I asked for it. When I finally entered recovery, Laurie was quick to reestablish a connection with me to begin rebuilding our relationship. Laurie understood judgment in a way that matters. She understood that genuine love and concern are far better ways to confront sin than judgment and condemnation.

Remember what I said about natural consequences to sin? It's OK to move people out of your inner circle. It's OK to change churches. It's OK not to call your sister on her birthday. It's even OK to say, "I can no longer trust you because you have proven yourself to be untrustworthy," and to never speak to someone again.

What's not OK is putting yourself in charge of inflicting punishment or exacting judgment on someone else.

One of the most difficult battles to surrender is the battle for justice. See, I think our judgment is often attached to a thirst for what's *right*. Somewhere along the way, we've been conditioned to believe that people should get what they deserve. This is as true for rewards as it is for punishments. So we place ourselves in the judge's chambers and we try to sentence others, often without even realizing what we're doing.

Unless you've been living in a remote cave with no access to the outside world, you've probably noticed that universal judgment is at an all-time high. The onset of the COVID-19 pandemic in 2020 ushered in an era of "I know what's best" to a degree that I've never personally witnessed in our culture. And, to be clear, our society was already serving up judgments like hotcakes. Arguments over masks, social distancing, medication, and vaccinations erupted into a cacophony of madness on social media and TV.

We may be in the medical field, we may be rocket scientists, we may be the smartest people on the planet. But you know what? We still aren't God. It's tempting to cast judgment on people for how they handled the pandemic (for which, by the way, there is still no widely read how-to guide) and all that followed. It's such an emotionally charged topic. But I wonder how many of us got quiet with God and asked him what he thought we should do—as individuals, as families, and as a country.

Do you know what I think Jesus would say to us? I think he would say that we're asking the wrong questions and we're fighting the wrong fight. See, Jesus is not concerned with our politics. He's concerned with our hearts.

Regardless of our stance, ideals, or convictions, we can find verses in the Bible that can be used to support our side of just about any argument. It happens when we come to the Bible looking for ways to prove a point regarding a belief system or action. We take it out of context or application really quickly. I know, because I've done it.

But if we took our judgments about political parties and COVID quarantines and mask and vaccination mandates to God, I think he'd point us to the two greatest commandments: "'Love the Lord your God with all your heart and with all your soul. Love him with all your mind.' This is the first and most important commandment. And the second is like it. 'Love your neighbor as you love yourself'" (Matt. 22:37–39).

If we say we are Christians, then we are Christ followers. And when we follow someone, we obey them. More than that, we imitate them. If we want to be obedient to Christ and want to be like Christ, we have to approach every single situation with this question: What does love require of me?[2]

The question is a good one because it points our hearts directly toward our true North—Jesus.

When it comes to mask mandates.

When it comes to vaccinations.

When it comes to how I respond on Facebook.

When it comes to how I respond on Instagram.

When it comes to how I position my heart toward people who think differently from me.

What does love require of me? The answer to that question applies not only to the choice you make personally but especially to your reaction to others' choices.

Brad and I have prayerfully navigated the pandemic and made choices for our family that haven't been popular with everyone. We've definitely been judged for our positions. Though I've wanted to at times, I don't get online and fight my battle with words. I don't forcefully share the reasons why we have chosen what we've chosen. I don't even really like to talk about it. Because honestly, I am not fit to be the Holy Spirit for every person who thinks differently from how I think.

When I get fired up, I have to pause. I have to ask myself, *What does love require of me?* And most often, love requires me to keep my mouth shut. It requires me to trust that everyone is acting on their own and their family's best interest. It requires me to acknowledge that not everyone is wired the way I'm wired. And to assume that people will handle catastrophic and unprecedented events the exact same way I do is actual lunacy.

To be clear, I'm not saying that following Jesus means we are all apolitical, becoming disinterested or apathetic when it comes to what's going on in our country. Definitely not. In fact, what I'm saying is quite the opposite. Being a follower of Jesus means that we think not along party lines but along Jesus lines. It means forming our opinions using the story and symbols of Jesus as our filter and guardrail. While we may vote one way, we should only follow *the Way*— according to his kingdom, his teaching, and his priorities— which are always, always based on love.

When I want to judge someone for their political position, the healthiest question I can ask is, What does love require of me?

Do you know what I've learned about judgmental people? Their judgment doesn't typically begin and end with others. Often, they are their own most cruel and critical judge. There's something about themselves that they don't accept or like or want. Maybe someone else's failures make them feel a little less aware of their own. But avoiding their own weaknesses causes so much suffering. So much. It makes them unaware or creates denial that leads to inauthenticity.

So if you're wondering where you can start with all of this, start with yourself. Forgive yourself. Let yourself off the hook. Deal with your issues honestly, but then move on from them. Relieve yourself of the suffering. Open your heart to the endless grace of Jesus—a grace he paid the ultimate price for and that saves you from all judgment, including your own.

10

Cure for the Common Craving

People are wise and understanding when they think
about the way they live.
But people are foolish when their foolish ways trick
them.

Proverbs 14:8

I'll never forget the first time someone broke up with me.
It was a guy in high school. I'm not sure what his reason was.
We dated for two years, y'all. Two *years*. I don't even think he
told me to my face. He told a friend to tell me or something
super mature like that. Anyway, it stung—obviously. Rejection
hurts, even if you really didn't want whatever it was to begin
with. I remember that afterward he tried to come back around
and talk to me again. I was like, "Nope. Had your chance."

This boy had the nerve to look at me and say, "Landra Young, I'm going to marry you."

This is the same guy who couldn't even break up with me over text like a normal teenager. I said, "No, you won't."

Once he knew he couldn't have me, he was hooked. He followed me around and begged me to get back together with him. But that's human nature, isn't it? We always want what we can't have.

That's how I feel right now, 732 weeks pregnant. I have honestly been pregnant or nursing for four straight years, and the list of things I can't have seems to get longer every day. Brad and I went to dinner the other night, and he got my favorite sushi roll. I didn't speak to him the entire way home. It was cruel! All I have thought about since that meal is how much I want raw, uncooked fish.

Have you ever fasted for Lent or for some other reason, and the very thing you fast from is all you want? I remember one year I gave up candy for Lent. I have such a sweet tooth, but I decided it was no big deal. I give up all kinds of things as a pregnant woman; I can do without candy. Then it seemed everywhere I looked—every commercial, billboard, and advertisement—it was all about milk chocolate with almonds or something like it.

We all know that feeling—that pull of seduction toward what we know we shouldn't or can't have. It's called temptation.

I think the most painful night of Jesus's life was in the garden of Gethsemane. The Bible tells us that Jesus was actually *sweating blood*. The next day, he faced the agony of the cross. That was Jesus's darkest day. But I think the darkest *season* of Jesus's life was when he was led to the wilderness to be tempted by the devil for forty days and nights.

I just want to go ahead and put this out there—none of us, including Jesus Christ, can avoid temptation. It is a struggle that *all* humankind faces. Temptation is not a sign of spiritual weakness. Many Christians are disgusted and demoralized by their own tendency to have tempting thoughts. We feel guilty that we aren't beyond or above being tempted. This is a misunderstanding of maturity. You will never outgrow temptation. Temptation is not a sign of weakness. More often than not, it is a sign of spiritual growth. In fact, a lot of times it means the enemy has noticed something about our walk with God that he doesn't like.

I know for me, when I worry about temptation, I am most aware of the "big" ones. You know, am I tempted to binge, am I tempted to purge, am I tempted to try to control things. These are some of the greatest temptations in my life. But they probably aren't the most detrimental temptations I've experienced. And the same is probably true for you. The most detrimental temptations are more insidious. They creep up on us—so much so that we aren't even aware of them.

You aren't tempted to go out and have this huge affair with a married person. You aren't tempted to get loaded and get behind the wheel of a car. You aren't tempted to embezzle thousands of dollars from your company. It's the smaller things: the temptation to gossip, the temptation to make excuses, the temptation to overspend. The small, seemingly harmless temptations that we face every day are the ones that cause us the most suffering.

If we want to become better, happier, and more stable, we have to learn to overcome temptation. But we can't learn how to overcome it until we understand it. The good news is that the author of temptation—the enemy—has zero new ideas.

He's used the same temptations over and over for thousands of years. Why? Because humans still fall for his same tricks. I know I do!

One word you hear a lot when it comes to temptation is to *resist*. We've been told that if we resist temptation, it'll go away. Well, I'm here to tell you that this just isn't true. It's a total fallacy. I can resist chocolate cake every single day, and the next time I see it, I'll still want chocolate cake.

Instead of resisting temptation, the goal should be to rethink temptation.

We talked briefly at the beginning of this book about the first ever temptation in Genesis 3. This is when the serpent (Satan) came to Eve and told her that she should break God's one and only rule and eat fruit from the forbidden tree. "You'll be just like God!" Satan told her. So Eve ate the fruit, marking the beginning of a pattern of giving in to temptation that humankind has perpetuated for years.

See, every temptation starts the same way. It starts with that tug—that pull toward what we know is wrong. Revenge. Greed. Lust. Or it can start with a good desire—to protect someone or show them love—but we go about acting on the desire in the wrong way or at the wrong time. Either way, temptation *starts* with a want. It starts with wanting something we don't have or have enough of.

You can be sure it's temptation when your mind keeps bringing it up. It starts to consume you. You think about it all the time. Your thoughts have gotten out of control because this temptation is the constant itch you're dying to scratch.

The next step in the pattern of temptation is when we doubt God's Word and his goodness. In Eve's case, it was when she believed Satan's whispered lies: Eating from that tree won't kill you. God's holding you back! You deserve to be like God! (Gen. 3:4–5).

After doubt, we try to deceive ourselves. We justify why we should get what we want. This is the third step in the pattern of temptation.

I work hard. I deserve some Lululemon.

My husband spends more time playing video games than he does with me. I deserve to be loved.

If I "borrow" a hundred bucks from petty cash, no one will notice it's gone. I put up with a lot around here—I deserve a little extra.

She gossips about everybody. She deserves to be gossiped about. Besides, it's not gossip if it's true, right?

It's not a blatant lie. It's mostly true. Who hasn't told a little white lie before?

It's not that bad. Nobody will find out.

The final step is when we disobey and cross over from temptation to sin.

The pattern is simple. We want something we don't have. We begin to doubt that God knows what's best for us or that he will provide it. So we justify what we want. We lie to ourselves (and often other people). And we succumb to temptation, which always gives way to sin.

Let me give you an example. When I was growing up, I was always tempted to bend the rules as long as I thought it wouldn't hurt anyone. I wasn't a rebel without a cause, blazing a trail of disobedience between church and home. I was more of a subtle rebel. I'd push at a boundary just to see how far I could take it. One of my parents' rules that I hated the most was that they took away our technology every school night at nine. This was a line that I was consistently tempted to cross.

One Thursday night, I really wanted to keep talking to my boyfriend later than my curfew allowed. I had an identical phone with a cracked screen that no longer had service connected to it. So when it was time to turn in our technology, I slipped the broken phone facedown onto my parents' nightstand and stayed up until the wee hours of Friday morning talking about that night's upcoming football game against our school's biggest rival. (In other words, nothing that mattered enough to break the rules over.)

The next morning, I got up and dressed for school quickly. I was so excited about the football game and seeing my boyfriend that I rushed out of the house. I was a few hours into the school day when my mom called me.

"Landra," she said calmly. "You'll need to come home right after school. You're grounded."

In my sleep-deprived and frenzied exit, I had forgotten to pocket the fake phone I'd left in their room. I wasn't allowed to go to the game, and I got my *real* phone privileges taken away for a long time. At that age, it was just about the worst punishment I could have imagined.

My thought process was typical of giving in to temptation. My desire was to talk to my boyfriend as long as I wanted. I began to doubt that my parents' motives for taking away our technology were valid. I deceived my parents by switching out the phones. I disobeyed and didn't even do a good job of it, busting myself by not removing the evidence.

Pastor Rick Warren puts it this way: "Desire leads to doubt leads to deception leads to disobedience."[1]

You have to be vigilant. You have to know yourself. You have to know where you're weak and where you're vulnerable. If I trace back all the times I've given in to temptation, you know the common denominator? My emotions. Anything difficult, sad, hard, depressing, or frustrating—when I'm in that pit of despair, the first thing I want to reach out to is the one that makes those feelings go away.

That was true for LeeBeth in her addiction. I don't think LeeBeth ever had a great day when she felt confident in God's love and favor that turned into a binge-drinking episode. No, they all originated in days and nights of negative feelings. Alcohol didn't reach down into the pit to help her out. Alcohol jumped down into the pit with her. Alcohol brought a glass and a shovel. While LeeBeth was numbing her rejection and fear, alcohol kept digging that pit deeper and deeper and deeper.

For me, I'm most tempted to return to old habits and addictions when I'm stressed out, when life feels too big and out of control. That's when I want to take matters into my own hands by way of my own coping mechanisms. And if I'm not vigilant, if I'm not guarding my heart and thoughts, I'll find myself with my head in the toilet, repeating past addictive behaviors.

So we've established that there's a pattern to temptation in general: desire, doubt, deception, and disobedience. But did you know that you have a pattern of temptation that's unique to you and your life? For example, my mom can sit in a Mexican restaurant and not dip a *single* chip into salsa and eat it. She can. I don't understand this self-control. It's a mystery to me. My toxic trait is to fill up on chips and salsa before my food even comes. My mom and I have very different temptation patterns.

What about you? When do you find yourself most vulnerable to temptation? There's a saying in recovery (and in counseling) that you ought to be conscious of your mood whenever you're feeling hungry, angry, lonely, or tired. The acronym is HALT—as in halt and think about what's really going on with your body and mind.

The *H* stands for hunger. Hunger can be either physical or emotional. You may be from a normal family, but in the Young and Hughes houses, if someone is hungry, it's past time to eat. I know other families who get together for meals and sit around in the kitchen and chat before eating. That is not our family. Feed us first, and then we can discuss the plans for Easter, OK? Sometimes, when we're angry or frustrated, the embarrassing truth is that we just need a cheeseburger.

Emotional hunger is another thing. We could be hungry for the attention of someone. We could be hungry for affirmation, success, or understanding. To abate these cravings, we sometimes turn to destructive habits or toxic relationships. But if we're careful to keep guard over our hearts, if we halt and think about what's really going on, we can identify the true hunger and bring it to God before giving in to temptation.

The *A* stands for anger. I think anger gets a bad rap. Some people think Jesus was never angry, but lots of things made him angry:

- Rules being placed over people (Matt. 12:10; John 9:16)
- Children being overlooked or undervalued (Matt. 18:14; 19:13–14; Mark 9:36–37)

- Self-righteousness and judgmentalism (Matt. 23:25–32)
- Making it difficult for people to get to God (Matt. 21:12–17; John 2:13–17)

Jesus was a rebel. I'm not sure there's been a rule breaker (not lawbreaker) like Jesus since Jesus. Of course, Jesus got angry. It's not a sin to be angry. But we're more likely to give in to the temptation to sin *because* of our anger if it goes unchecked.

If you're feeling especially miffed, punch a pillow. Practice breathing techniques. Meditate. Exercise. There are healthy ways to handle and manage your anger. But whatever you do, don't dismiss or ignore it.

The *L* stands for loneliness. We've already touched on this topic. Loneliness can strike whether we're all alone or surrounded by many people. It can also be self-inflicted and is almost always self-perpetuated. If you're experiencing loneliness right now, ask yourself honestly, *Why haven't I reached out to someone?* Loneliness is a trigger for just about every negative coping mechanism I can think of. There are counselors, pastors, and support groups (online and in person) available, so you really don't have an excuse to *stay* lonely.

Finally, the *T* stands for tiredness. Y'all, I've been tired for four years. I'm about to have three kids under five years old. I think this is just who I am right now—tired. The problem with our society is that we accept being tired as a by-product of our lifestyle. But that's not how we're supposed to live. Even Jesus took opportunities to rest during his ministry on earth.

This isn't news to any of us, but we're not Jesus. So if Jesus required rest, we require rest. Sometimes the dishes are left in the sink. Sometimes the ministry event gets run by someone else. Sometimes it's OK to let the kids sleep over at your in-laws. Maybe they'll come home sleep-deprived and sugar-filled, but parenting isn't about perfection. Recharging your mind, your body, and your spirit will help you avoid the pitfalls of giving in to temptation.

I can assure you that even if you aren't aware of your personal temptation pattern, Satan is. Proverbs 14:8 tells us why recognizing our own patterns is important:

> People are wise and understanding when they think
> about the way they live.
> But people are foolish when their foolish ways
> trick them.

We have to think about and evaluate how we live. We have to face the facts about our own temptation patterns. Mature people are self-aware. Knowing where you're weak doesn't make you weak—it makes you strong. It prepares you. It's preemptive. You can say no to temptation before you're actually tempted. For example, I can't take Sterling into Target anymore. She begs for toys—*begs*. And I get it. Target is magical. I want "toys" from Target too (clothes, candles, every furry blanket they've ever sold). But the temptation for her to get a new toy is so great, I preemptively just don't take her anymore. The little no before the big no is always the easier one.

Ask yourself the following:

- *What do I wish I'd stop doing?* Maybe you wish you'd stop breaking your diet. Maybe you wish you'd stop gossiping. Maybe you wish you'd stop overspending.

- *When am I most tempted?* Are you most tempted to snap at your family in the mornings? Are you most tempted to send a flirtatious text to a coworker late at night?

- *Where am I most tempted?* Are you most tempted at the mall? At work? At the gym? In the kitchen?

- *Who am I with when I'm most tempted?* Are you usually alone when you give in to temptation? Or is there typically someone else involved?

- *What temporary benefit do I get when I give in?* If there wasn't some pleasure or fun involved, you wouldn't be tempted to do it. What fix or high is giving in to your temptation providing you with? Even if you hate yourself or feel immediate regret or remorse after giving in, there is some sort of payout or you wouldn't feel pulled toward it.

All these questions or assessments may seem overboard. But the Bible tells us this level of self-awareness isn't over-analysis, it's wisdom. Proverbs 4:26 says, "Think carefully about the paths that your feet walk on." In other words, make a plan to walk in accordance with God's will. Make a plan to *avoid* falling into temptation.

See, when we fall *into* temptation, we don't just fall out. That would be nice, right? But that's not how it works. We have to *climb out* of temptation. I don't know about you, but I'm not much for climbing. I have friends who go hiking all the time, and they love it. Don't get me wrong—I love to get outside and walk and sometimes even run (when I'm not growing a human inside my body). But I'm not sure why anyone in their right mind would choose to endure an uphill battle. That's why it's called an uphill *battle.* You're working at it the entire time with no reprieve from the labor. Rock climbing or uphill hiking of any kind is just not in my nature. And I don't think it's in anyone's nature to choose the uphill battle of climbing out of temptation.

Just like you need the right gear to climb the face of a mountain, you need the right gear to climb out of temptation. It requires work. It requires tools. It requires discipline. It may mean you go to an AA meeting or Celebrate Recovery. It may mean you need an accountability partner or a prayer partner. It may even mean you need to change jobs or stop hanging around certain people or stop going places or stop following Instagram accounts.

Let's look at how Jesus handled his season of temptation:

Jesus, full of the Holy Spirit, left the Jordan River. The Spirit led him into the desert. There the devil tempted him for 40 days. Jesus ate nothing during that time. At the end of the 40 days, he was hungry.

The devil said to him, "If you are the Son of God, tell this stone to become bread."

Jesus answered, "It is written, 'Man must not live only on bread.'" (Luke 4:1–4)

The very first sentence reveals the most important and useful tool available to anyone who is in Christ—his *Holy Spirit.* Now, I know the topic of the Holy Spirit can make people feel a little weird. We're good with God. We can even accept that Jesus is God manifested in the flesh. But the Holy Spirit? The "holy ghost"? We can get a little freaked out about that.

John 14:26 says, "But the Father will send the Friend in my name to help you. The Friend is the Holy Spirit. He will teach you all things. He will remind you of everything I have said to you."

That "Friend" we're promised is the Spirit of God. If it helps you understand it better to say "Spirit of God" instead of "Holy Spirit," by all means call him the Spirit of God. Because that's who the Holy Spirit is. The Spirit of God is that still, small voice in your gut, in your heart, in the back of your mind—wherever you feel his presence. That's the Holy Spirit. Just as in any relationship, the more awareness you have of his presence, the more that presence will grow, the easier it becomes to discern his voice and his guidance in your life, and the more likely you are to overcome temptation.

The Bible doesn't just say that Jesus entered the wilderness *with* the Holy Spirit. It says he was *filled* with the Holy Spirit. In other words, the battle stations of his mind and heart were manned. Jesus was prepared for the uphill climb of resisting temptation. And if Jesus needs the Holy Spirit to overcome temptation, I'd say it's a safe bet that we do too.

The question is, How do we get the Holy Spirit? We ask for him. We listen to him. Remember, the more we listen, the deeper our awareness of his presence. The more obedience we show to his call, the more likely we are to hear that call again in the future. You want more of the Holy Spirit? Be responsive to the portion you have right now—in the big things and in the small things too. We get offtrack from his guidance when we become *overfull* of our own wisdom and knowledge—when we rely too much on ourselves and our own understanding.

Paul warns against trusting in ourselves in Philippians 3:

> We don't put our trust in who we are or what we can do. I have many reasons to trust in who I am and what I have done. Someone else may think they have reasons to trust in these things. But I have even more.
>
> I was circumcised on the eighth day. I am part of the people of Israel. I am from the tribe of Benjamin. I am a pure Hebrew. As far as the law is concerned, I am a Pharisee. As far as being committed is concerned, I opposed and attacked the church. As far as keeping the law is concerned, I kept it perfectly. (vv. 3–6)

Paul says if anyone could justify putting their trust in themselves, it was him. He was circumcised like a good Jew. He was from the right area, from a good family. He kept the law perfectly. But then he went on to say:

> I thought things like that were really something great. But now I consider them to be nothing because of Christ. Even more, I consider everything to be nothing compared to knowing Christ Jesus my Lord. To know him is worth much more than anything else. Because of him I have lost everything. But I consider all of it to be garbage so I can know Christ better. I want to be joined to him. Being right with God does not come from my obeying the law. It comes because I believe in Christ. It comes from God because of faith. I want to know Christ better. Yes, I want to know the power that raised him from the dead. (vv. 7–10)

After coming to know Jesus Christ, Paul realized that being "right" or "good" meant nothing. He realized that knowing Jesus, regardless of the cost, was all that mattered. And knowing him has *nothing* to do with behaving well. It has nothing to do with what family you come from or where you're born. Knowing him, relying on him, being in constant communication with his Spirit, having a growing faith of your own—that's how to become "right" with God. That's how you climb out of temptation the way Jesus did.

There's a part of Philippians 3 we'd like to skim over or leave off. It comes in verses 10–11: "I want to join him in his sufferings. I want to become like him by sharing in his death. Then by God's grace I will rise from the dead."

If we say we want to follow Christ, that means two things. First, we share in his sufferings. Part of Christ's torment was that season of temptation in the wilderness. It also includes all the suffering we've already talked about in this book. So to share in Christ's narrative is synonymous with suffering of all kinds. Suffering is the bare minimum expectation of every Christian.

And second, we share in his death—death of our pride, death of our ego, death of our will, death of our way. When we do this, when we die to ourselves by putting our faith in Christ, then by his grace we are given eternity in heaven. Sounds like a pretty good deal if you're looking at it from a cost-to-outcome perspective. We give up what we want, we trade it for what God wants (which is always better), and in the end, we get to live forever in paradise. Sign me up!

Ephesians 6:11–18 summarizes our best strategy against temptation:

Put on all of God's armor. Then you can remain strong against the devil's evil plans. Our fight is not against human beings. It is against the rulers, the authorities and the powers of this dark world. It is against the spiritual forces of evil in the heavenly world. So put on all of God's armor. Evil days will come. But you will be able to stand up to anything. And after you have done everything you can, you will still be standing. So remain strong in the faith. Put the belt of truth around your waist. Put the armor of godliness on your chest. Wear on your feet what will prepare you to tell the good news of peace. Also, pick up the shield of faith. With it you can put out all the flaming arrows of the evil one. Put on the helmet of salvation. And take the sword of the Holy Spirit. The sword is God's word.

At all times, pray by the power of the Spirit. Pray all kinds of prayers. Be watchful, so that you can pray. Always keep on praying for all the Lord's people.

You may have heard it said that we are in a spiritual battle. I believe that's true. And I believe the enemy is real. But I also believe that *we* can be an enemy to ourselves if we fail to enter life's greatest temptations without the right protection—the full armor of God.

How does this struggle play out for me right now? The temptations are almost too many to count. I'm tempted to blame God for taking LeeBeth from us. Why would he choose her? She wasn't a drug addict with a syringe in her arm. She wasn't abusive, mean, or evil. With all the murderers and rapists alive today, why did he choose to take LeeBeth instead?

I'm tempted to blame my parents. To blame myself. To blame LeeBeth. To blame alcohol. To blame the guy who broke her heart. The temptation to place blame weighs heavily. I'm still in the middle of climbing my way out of it.

I'm tempted to give up in the middle of my grief journey—to give in to it and to just stop living well and enjoying life. People say that over time your grief gets smaller. I haven't found that to be true. For me, it seems life tends to grow bigger around my grief. But my grief is always there, never changing shape or size.

Every day, I want to be like Paul. I want to share in the sufferings of Jesus because I want to know *him*. But it's hard. I can't do it without the power of the Holy Spirit. I can't do it without prayer. I can't do it without community. I just keep putting put one foot in front of the other. Often, that's all I have the strength to do. That may be one foot toward the bed, one foot toward the altar, one foot toward my counselor.

What I can tell you is that every step I take away from temptation is one step away from the mess of sin and one step closer to Jesus.

EPILOGUE

I miss LeeBeth every day.

I am a different person since losing her. I am riding the waves of emotions daily, sometimes hourly. I cling desperately to my life preserver—Jesus.

If nothing more, LeeBeth's life reminds us that our lives on earth are not the end of the story, and how we choose to live them is our gift of service to God.

Grief is strange—it's the messiest of messes. It's given me such a deep appreciation for people who lose someone. In the past, when I would hear of a loss, I'd think to myself, *Oh, gosh, I'll pray for them.* And I meant it in the moment but would maybe follow through once or twice before their grief became a distant memory. Now? Now I long for people to remember.

I want them to remember LeeBeth and remember us in prayer. Because even though it's been some time since we lost her, some mornings I wake up and it feels like it just happened. I miss her so much that I can't move. I don't want to talk to anyone or see anyone. There are other days that

I'm angry. I'm like a wet hornet and anyone in my path gets stung. I'm mad at LeeBeth. I'm mad at God. I'm mad at the world.

Some days I grieve who she really was. I grieve who I thought she was. I grieve who she never got to be. And then the next day, I'll be OK. I'll even feel fine. I can talk about her and look at pictures of her. Honestly, grief over death is as unpredictable as the life that precedes it. There are no guarantees. There is no road map. There is no measure. The only solid security found in all these moments—that sometimes even overlap—is God, Jesus, and the Holy Spirit. The love and grace and healing hands of my Father in heaven.

My grief may change, but God never does.

In an interview for a Church Leaders article, my dad said something that I absolutely love. He talked about how it was hard for him "not to seek an explanation for why this tragedy happened." But he added that, "As believers, we don't stand on explanations. We stand on the promises of God. And that is so, so important."[1]

If God explained all our disappointments to us, I still don't think it would take away our pain. That leads me to believe that our pain has purpose. And that purpose is to make us more like him and draw us closer to him.

Yes, there is pain. Yes, there are struggles. But each experience, each disappointment, hurt, and battle, are refining us. They're improving us. I think in some ways, our own pain heals us.

And I'd like to think pain brings me closer to LeeBeth too. Yes, LeeBeth had her faults and shortcomings. She was a pistol, full of mischief and ideas. But she was *his*. She was loved by God and by her family. And when she was healthy, she pursued the heart of God like no one else I know. In its own way, getting closer to God has to get me closer to LeeBeth.

I ran into one of the students LeeBeth pastored when she was in charge of our PK Vacay camp. PK Vacay is for kids of pastors—from sixth graders to high school graduates. Being a pastor's kid is what my dad would call "brutiful"—both brutal and beautiful at the same time. But LeeBeth understood the call of a PK better than most.

The student said to me, "I'm sorry to hear about LeeBeth. She made me feel like everything was going to be OK."

In the moment, I'm sure I made some blanket statement, thanking the student and wishing them the best. But in hindsight, I think that statement pretty much sums up LeeBeth. She had this faithful optimism that made it seem like everything really was going to be OK.

Every loss.

Every heartbreak.

Every death.

Every disappointment.

Every struggle.

With hope in our powerful, loving, and lavishly generous God, she knew that it was all going to be OK.

LeeBeth loved the show *The Office*. I personally have a hard time watching it. I mean, I get that it's hilarious, but those peak-cringe moments are too much for me to watch. I can't do it! Every time I'd hang out at her house, she'd have *The Office* playing in the background, even if we weren't watching TV.

I asked LeeBeth once what her favorite episode was, and she answered immediately, "Oh, the one where Michael Scott leaves. He moves to marry the girl he loves."

I remember thinking at the time how weird that was. To love an episode of a show where the main character moves away. But now when I think about LeeBeth's response, I smile. LeeBeth was a selfless dreamer who wanted everyone to get their happy ending. And that's what Michael Scott got—forever with the love of his life. It may have cost the viewers their comedic relief, leading man, and main story line, but it gave him a happy ending that LeeBeth loved.

That's how I picture LeeBeth now.

It cost God a great deal—his Son—but she got her happy ending. She's forever with the one who loves her most.

NOTES

Chapter 2 Isolation Station

1. Amy Novotney, "The Risks of Social Isolation," *American Psychological Association* 50, no. 5 (May 2019), https://www.apa.org/monitor/2019/05/ce-corner-isolation.

2. Rick McDaniel, "God May Have Put You in a Lonely Place for an Incredible Reason," Fox News, July 9, 2018, https://www.foxnews.com/opinion/god-may-have-put-you-in-a-lonely-place-for-an-incredible-reason.

Chapter 3 What a Girl Wants

1. "The Twelve Steps," Step 1, Alcoholics Anonymous, accessed March 24, 2022, https://www.aa.org/the-twelve-steps.

2. "The Twelve Steps," Step 2.

3. Henry W. F. Saggs, "Nebuchadnezzar II," *Encyclopedia Britannica*, November 5, 2019, https://www.britannica.com/biography/Nebuchadnezzar-II.

4. "Nebuchadnezzar," Shmoop, accessed March 24, 2022, https://www.shmoop.com/study-guides/bible/daniel/nebuchadnezzar.

Chapter 4 Do I Smell Something Burning?

1. "Burn Incidence Fact Sheet," American Burn Association, accessed February 1, 2022, https://ameriburn.org/who-we-are/media/burn-incidence-fact-sheet/.

2. George Anders, "Burnout Signs Have Risen 33% in 2020; Here Are Seven Ways to Reduce Risks," LinkedIn, October 8, 2020, https://www.linkedin.com/pulse/burnout-signs-have-risen-33-2020-here-seven-ways-reduce-george-anders.

3. Gretchen Livingston and Deja Thomas, "Among 41 Countries, Only U.S. Lacks Paid Parental Leave," Pew Research Center, December 16, 2019, https://www.pewresearch.org/fact-tank/2019/12/16/u-s-lacks -mandated-paid-parental-leave/.

4. Livingston and Thomas, "Among 41 Countries."

Chapter 5 Hurts So Good

1. Isobel Whitcomb, "Why Does 'Emotional Pain' Hurt?," Live Science, May 10, 2021, https://www.livescience.com/why-emotional-pain -hurts.html.

2. Whitcomb, "Why Does 'Emotional Pain' Hurt?"

3. Ethan Kross et al., "Social Rejection Shares Somatosensory Representations with Physical Pain," PNAS, April 12, 2011, https://www.pnas .org/content/108/15/6270.

Chapter 6 We All Fall Down

1. "Is Addiction Really a Disease?," Indiana University Health, December 30, 2011, https://iuhealth.org/thrive/is-addiction-really-a-disease.

2. "Drugs and the Brain," National Institute on Drug Abuse, July 2020, https://nida.nih.gov/publications/drugs-brains-behavior-science -addiction/drugs-brain.

3. "Drugs and the Brain."

4. The content to follow was inspired by Erick Schenkel, "5 Biblical Characters Who Prove That Failure Isn't Fatal," Jesus Film Project, accessed March 24, 2022, https://www.jesusfilm.org/blog-and-stories/is-failure-fatal.html.

5. Joni Eareckson Tada, "God Permits What He Hates," joni&friends, May 15, 2013, https://old.joniandfriends.org/radio/4-minute/god-permits -what-he-hates1/.

Chapter 7 Slaying the Giant

1. Jon Bloom, "Why Jesus Wept," desiringGod, April 29, 2011, https:// www.desiringgod.org/articles/why-jesus-wept.

2. "Forgiveness: Your Health Depends on It," Johns Hopkins Medicine, accessed February 1, 2022, https://www.hopkinsmedicine.org/health /wellness-and-prevention/forgiveness-your-health-depends-on-it.

Chapter 8 Trees of Life

1. "What Does It Mean That Hope Deferred Makes the Heart Sick (Proverbs 13:12)?," Got Questions, accessed March 24, 2022, https://www .gotquestions.org/hope-deferred.html.

2. "What Does It Mean That Hope Deferred Makes the Heart Sick?"

3. Quoted in Amanda Enayati, "How Hope Can Help You Heal," CNN Health, updated April 11, 2013, https://www.cnn.com/2013/04/11/health/hope-healing-enayati/index.html.

4. "What Does It Mean That Hope Deferred Makes the Heart Sick?"

Chapter 9 I Have an Opinion, Your Honor

1. "Number of Monthly Active Facebook Users Worldwide as of 4th Quarter 2021," Statista, accessed March 8, 2020, https://www.statista.com/statistics/264810/number-of-monthly-active-facebook-users-worldwide/.

2. I'd like to take credit for wordsmithing the question that well, but Pastor Andy Stanley of North Point Community Church in Alpharetta, Georgia, actually coined it in his Brand: New series, "Part 4: What Love Requires," February 22, 2015, https://northpoint.org/messages/brand-new/what-love-requires.

Chapter 10 Cure for the Common Craving

1. Rick Warren, "How to Overcome Persistent Temptations," YouTube video, posted by Saddleback Church, March 25, 2019, https://www.youtube.com/watch?v=LkvR9Vgr9uk.

Epilogue

1. Jessica Lea, "Ed and Lisa Share LeeBeth's Cause of Death, How God Has Been Faithful," Church Leaders, February 16, 2021, https://churchleaders.com/news/390338-leebeth-young-death-faithful.html/.

Landra Young Hughes is the daughter of prominent pastors Ed Young Jr. and Lisa Young of Fellowship Church. Because of her upbringing, Landra has developed a passion for seeing people maximize their God-given potential and embracing their God-defined self-worth. She and her husband, Brad, serve on staff at Fellowship Church's Grapevine campus and live in Dallas, Texas, with their daughter, Sterling, and their sons, Jackson and Bear.

Holly Crawshaw is a writer, editor, and writing coach who is passionate about partnering with authors to leverage their stories for good. Holly is raising three daughters, Lilah (the silly one), Esmae (the charming one), and Sailor (the sweet one) in her hometown outside of Atlanta, Georgia.

CONNECT WITH
LANDRA

Journey together with Landra
to embrace your God-defined self-worth
and overcome grief and adversity.

FIND HER ONLINE

LandraYoungHughes   LandraHughes

www.FellowshipChurch.com and www.LandraHughes.com

CHOOSE TO LET GOD'S LOVE DEFINE YOU

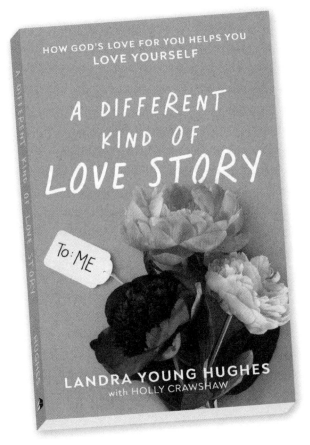

If you've ever struggled with your identity, Landra Young Hughes has a radically simple message for you: give up. Out of her own deeply personal story of trying to control her circumstances and others' perceptions of her through an eating disorder, Landra points the way toward a life free from self-obsession and self-resentment. She shows you how to listen to God's voice, let go of the struggle for perfection, and live authentically from your deepest self.

Connect with
BakerBooks
Relevant. Intelligent. Engaging.

Sign up for announcements about
new and upcoming titles at

BakerBooks.com/SignUp

@ReadBakerBooks

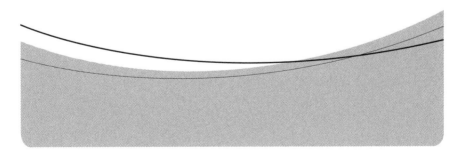